D0492382

Garden lighting

hamlyn

Garden lighting

John Raine

First published in Great Britain in
2001 by Hamlyn,
a division of Octopus Publishing
Group Limited,
2–4 Heron Quays,
London E14 4JP

This paperback edition
published in 2005

Copyright © 2001, 2005 Octopus
Publishing Group Limited

All rights reserved.
No part of this publication may be
reproduced, stored in a retrieval
system, or transmitted, in any
form or by any means, electronic,
electrostatic, magnetic tape,
mechanical, photocopying, record-
ing or otherwise, without
the prior permission in writing
of the publisher.

ISBN 0 600 61285 6
EAN 97806006612858

British Library Cataloguing
-in-Publication Data
A catalogue record for this book is
available from the British Library

Printed and bound in China
10 9 8 7 6 5 4 3 2 1

In describing all the projects
in this book, every care has
been taken to recommend the
safest methods of working.
Before starting any task,
you should be confident that
you know what you are doing,
and that you know how to
use equipment safely. The
publishers cannot accept any
legal responsibility or liability
for accidents or damage
arising from carrying out
the projects in this book.

contents

Introduction

above: Illumination is provided by hidden light sources so the beauty of the garden scene is not compromised by the obvious presence of lighting hardware.

The basic function of lighting is to extend the hours in the day. Recent developments in lighting technology have encouraged us to look at how light sources are used as an integral part of the overall design, first in our homes and now in our gardens. The wider choice of products available lately, especially energy-saving and compact models, has made the addition of lighting to the garden both practical and affordable, and the increased use of lighting in public spaces has provided inspirational examples of how light can enhance or completely alter the appearance of buildings and structures. Increasingly, we see the garden as an extension of our indoor living space, and introducing lighting there will not only extend the time you can spend outdoors but will also give it a quite different appearance.

Outdoor rooms

Interest in both interior and garden design has increased during the last few years, and the desire to make the most of our personal space has been heightened by exposure to the makeover industry on television and in print. A garden provides valuable extra space, and using it as an outdoor room is an idea that has grown in popularity, even where it is sometimes too cool or wet for night-time al fresco dining. Simply placing a table and chairs on a patio outside the french windows has developed into a more elaborate arrangement, and outdoor cooking, eating, entertainment and relaxation now require a range of convenient services.

The outdoor room is now a concept central to garden design, and it is perhaps this more than anything else that has promoted a demand for stylish outdoor lighting. The barbecue area, patios, structures for shade and shelter, statuary and planting can be enhanced by lighting that goes beyond the bright, functional output of a wall-mounted bulkhead light or floodlight. A garden that has been 'designed' – that is, one that has focal points, structure in its layout, good planting and a sense of perspective –

is more likely to benefit from lighting design. This need not mean a design undertaken by a professional garden designer or landscape architect – far from it, many amateur designs are inspired landscapes.

above: The uplighting of the small ornamental tree is framed by latticework columns which are illuminated by internally-mounted spotlights to create a more three-dimensional scene.

Reversing the daylight effect

Daylight means that everything in the garden and its surroundings is visible, because it is all lit by the sun. This is as true for a bare shed, neighbouring houses or power lines behind your prized statue as it is for the pleasing features within the garden. When night falls, however, lighting can be used to

below: The ornamental lighting of decorative trelliswork, statue and water feature are complemented by terrace lighting, which can be controlled by a separate switch to cater for different uses of this 'outdoor' room.

Taking theatre into the garden

Many techniques used in creative garden lighting derive from theatre lighting, where they include creating atmosphere, moulding a backdrop for the players or even reinforcing the character of certain players, altering the perception of time and season, and changing the perspective itself so that the same set is viewed in contrasting ways for different scenes. Theatre lighting is relatively powerful, and many of the tricks, such as subtly coloured gels, and beam control devices such as barn doors, are not easily weatherproofed at a smaller scale for exterior use. However, subtle theatrical effects can be achieved in the garden with miniaturized, low power, light sources that create focused beams of light.

Practicality and creativity

A creative garden lighting scheme does not mean that you have to ignore or compromise the need for functional lighting. In homes and gardens, lighting is needed for safe access, security and

above: Recessed uplights placed close to the base of the rocks emphasize the surface texture, as well as revealing colour and shape against the dark backdrop of unlit trees.

right: An illuminated statue provides a beautiful focal point in a garden.

take control of what is seen. Apart from the effects of moonlight or skyglow in the city, the rule is 'if you don't light it you won't see it'. Dramatic directional lighting will provide a contrast to the saturated downlighting of daylight, giving opportunities to create a fantasy scene by lighting water features and focal points, graceful trees and architectural plants. Outdoor lighting can be more dramatic than interior illumination because most gardens are larger than any room. In addition to providing a visual panorama in the garden, lighting changes the way that an outdoor space is used. Entertaining on the patio or around the swimming pool, or just enjoying the expanse of the night sky overhead, become priorities when the weather warms up. Garden lighting will encourage al fresco activity by lighting paths and patios, and combining ornamental and functional lighting can change the feel of such areas to create a totally different experience.

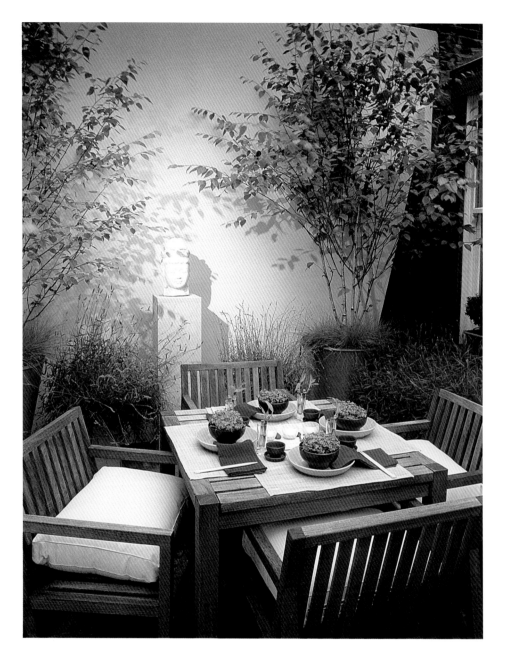

such essential functions as transferring children and shopping from car to house. Al fresco dining is only the start of this story: task lighting to cook by, lighting to enable us to appreciate the appearance of food as well as its aroma and flavour and amenity lighting to avoid tumbling down the steps from the kitchen are essential. In the dining room the ceiling and walls provide lighting platforms for illuminating the table, the décor and art works. Outside where there is no ceiling and there are probably fewer walls, substituting fresh air for interior décor demands alternative ways of creating interest in the surroundings, whether it be a panorama around the garden or the 'furnishings' within – planting, focal points, decorative paving or the sparkle of water. When the sun sets, creative garden lighting comes into its own.

Creative garden lighting

Creative garden lighting concentrates on subtle schemes that create atmosphere and enhance the planting, garden features and architecture,

above: Spotlighting the stone head provides a focal point amongst the general illumination of this al fresco dining area.

providing stimulating night-time vistas. One thing to remember is that the choice of light fittings comes last, not first. The aim is to create a beautifully illuminated garden where the light fittings are kept invisible as far as possible and where there is no glare from unshielded light sources at night. It is the visual effects that matter, not the light fittings – who wants their visitors to exclaim at the light fittings rather than the specimen plants, the graceful statue or the serenity of the garden as a whole?

The design approach

The creative use of light and shadow is the key to achieving good results, as only this will give depth and true

right: Uplighting a statue against a dark background creates a focal point with stronger impact than it has in daylight.

below: Uplighting a mature tree adds vertical drama to the night-time view of the illuminated garden.

interest in the view. Excessive lighting and the indiscriminate use of floodlights are common errors that result in garish illumination and a 'flat' perspective. 'Painting with light' is the term often used to describe the techniques, although it is used in the artistic, selective sense rather than in the bland task of covering a wall. Creative garden lighting is concerned with illuminating features to exploit texture, form and colour in order to suggest a sense of depth. Combinations of light and shadow can create dramatic effects that are in complete contrast to the daylight scene.

Garden lighting can be all the more magical if the garden design has taken its use into account from the start in the choice of features, materials and viewpoints. Just as good garden design will marry house to garden, so must the lighting. Downlighting on a terrace can be combined with subtle façade lighting to link the terrace and house, while the lighting for the front garden or drive should interpret the appearance of, and show the route through, the front of the property, as well as providing a welcoming focus for visitors when they arrive at the front door.

Designing a lighting system

A creative lighting system is only partly a question of choosing the areas and features to light: it also involves a consideration of layout, function and practicality. Selecting lighting subjects and techniques can never be divorced from the different uses of the garden, or parts of it, at night. For instance, a security light without a manual control switch would be inappropriate in an area with decorative lighting, and terrace wall lights are better if controlled by a different switch from the ornamental lighting circuit. Unless they have been chosen specifically to make a design statement – by an entrance, for example – light fittings need to be hidden or camouflaged wherever possible, so ones that are recessed, small or in a finish that blends in with the surroundings (or all three) are desirable. Good lighting

design depends fundamentally upon correct positioning and on selecting the correct lamp type, wattage and coverage or beam angle.

This book aims to guide you through the whole design process, starting with explanations of some relevant lighting terminology and the types of light fittings available, progressing through the ways in which different types of lighting can be used around the garden and including an explanation of the lighting effects that can be achieved. The choice of lighting fittings and the methods for controlling lighting are described, and there is practical advice on how to implement designs. The emphasis throughout is on using lighting techniques with a professional standard of equipment and design to produce a truly impressive result. This book will appeal to homeowners who aspire to having creative lighting design in their gardens, but it will also provide a comprehensive introduction to the subject for garden and landscape designers and contractors.

below: A combination of lighting under the bridge, underwater lighting and uplighting of the waterfalls brings this scene to life after dark.

Lamps and lighting

above: Choosing small light sources permits the use of luminaires hidden discreetly among planting and landscape features.

Visible light is the light that our eyes detect, and the aim of artificial lighting is, on the whole, to provide conditions that approximate to natural light, so that we can see objects at night as we do during the day. To introduce a lighting system into your garden, you do not need to know that visible light is one of the types of radiation in the electro-magnetic spectrum; nor do you need to know that the visible light spectrum ranges through the colours of the rainbow. It will be helpful, however, if you understand the properties of light that affect the way that artificial light can be used. If you appreciate how these properties can be used and exploited within your garden, lighting design can become truly creative.

Light, lamps and luminaires

The terminology used to describe lights and lighting can be confusing. It has developed in a haphazard way and is defined differently in professional and in day-to-day usage. In addition, it varies from country to country. In this book the following terms are used.

• **Light** is a visual phenomenon; it is the beam or glow that is emitted by a lamp.

• **Lamp** is the source of light. It is commonly (if imprecisely) referred to as a 'light bulb', but the word can also apply to a tube, globe, reflector lamp and capsule.

• **Luminaire** is the housing or body containing the holder or socket of a light source or lamp.

Measures of light

Light levels in the garden at night contrast sharply with daylight levels: the brightest moonlight has only a fraction of the intensity of direct sunlight, but even at this level the human eye can perceive shape, colour and detail, and it is generally the minimum level for pathlighting domestic gardens. Against the background of such low ambient light levels in the garden at night, it is no surprise that even low levels of lighting achieve dramatic results.

The standard measure of output for lamps is called a lumen. The amount of illumination that a lamp provides is measured in lux, which is the number of lumens per square metre. Bright moonlight is 1–2 lux. In North America the term 'footcandle' is used. One footcandle is equal to about 10 lux. In lamps with reflectors, it is the intensity of the beam that matters, and that is measured in candelas.

Brightness

In creative garden lighting it is always important to avoid glare, which will instantly ruin an otherwise well-lit scene. Brightness and glare, however, are two sides of the same coin. A beam of light does not necessarily stop at the subject on which it is focused, and poorly positioned lighting or the wrong choice of lamp beam or wattage can result in light straying in unwanted directions to produce glare. A common mistake is to place luminaires with over-bright lamps near a front door in the belief that bright lighting is always good lighting. Although a high level of lighting is often intended to help the home-owner identify a visitor, lighting the person rather than the entrance and its approach is intimidating rather than welcoming, because it produces glare at eye level. The light itself becomes the focus of attention rather than the area or object that it is meant to illuminate.

Glare

Glare from the wrong kind of lighting is as bad as no lighting at all. There are two main types of glare.

• **Discomfort glare** is the name given to the type of light in which it is possible to perform a desired function but with some degree of discomfort. We have to squint through the glare towards an object or shield our eyes with a hand in order to see the illuminated area below or beyond the glare.

• **Disability glare** is the term for the light in which normal vision is impossible, and

below: Illumination of the garden scene should ensure that glare from the chosen luminaires is eliminated.

we may even become disoriented because nothing useful is visible. It is often the result of unexpected exposure to very bright lighting and is the theory behind security floodlighting.

Distance and angle of light

The amount of light we choose to shine from a light fitting towards an object is only the starting point and other factors, including distance and the angle of the light, must also be considered. The apparent brightness of light falling on an object is affected by a number of factors. The farther away the lamp is from the subject, the brighter the light source must be to achieve the same effect. A further variable is the angle at which the light strikes a surface. If a circular beam is directed at right angles to a wall it will provide a circle of light of a given level. If the light strikes the same surface at the same distance from the same lamp but from a different angle, however, the same amount of light is spread over a larger, oval area. The light level is reduced by a factor relating to the angle at which the light strikes the surface. In addition, our perception of the brightness of light depends to some extent on what other lighting is around it: a single accent light will appear brighter if there is little ambient light than if there are other similar areas of light nearby. This is because the human eye adapts to light and dark by opening and closing the iris. This may all seem complicated, but in succeeding chapters we will see how flexibility in a lighting design will allow us to experiment with, and customize, the lighting effect.

Reflectance

The word reflectance is used to describe the percentage of light reflected from a surface. Dark colours reflect much less light than lighter colours and also absorb more light than they reflect. Rough surfaces scatter light and significantly reduce the amount reflected towards the eye compared to smooth surfaces. The box on page 15 indicates the reflectance of various materials common in gardens and the practical implications when choosing which lamp power to use. The concept may seem academic, but the result is practical – for example, what brightness of lamp do you need to light a white marble statue in your garden and how is this light requirement affected if you replace it with a dark bronze subject?

Choosing lamps

Good lighting is fundamentally about choosing the right lamp for the job. The lamp, traditionally known as a 'light bulb', provides an all-round light output appropriate for lighting around a patio, illuminating the route from the car to the house or providing lighting around the front door. Wall lights are typical uses for tungsten 'light bulbs'. Tubular and compact fluorescent lamps and many of the types used in street lighting come into this category of light sources; they provide an all-round light that diffuses in all directions unless controlled or directed by an external reflector. Garden lighting is principally about creating effects, and it requires a considerable degree of control and

below: Uplighting the apple tree complements the 'moonlighting' of the path meandering alongside it. The overall impression is a mellow one, suited to the ambience of an out-of-town garden, and results from choosing low-voltage, wide-angle lamps.

direction of the light source. Creative garden lighting cannot generally be achieved by diffusion light sources; instead, we use reflector lamps. These are lamps that use a reflective coating or a shaped mirror surface to project a controlled beam of light. Only a few diffusion light sources are used in garden lighting, including metal halide lamps, and their small size makes them suitable for use with external reflectors to produce controlled beams of light.

Colour rendering

We take the natural colour of daylight for granted and assume that artificial lighting should strive to match it, a phenomenon known as colour rendering. Lamps are rated on a scale out of 100, and the higher the number the more natural the lit subject appears – 80+ out of 100, for instance, means the light provides good colour rendering. Colour rendering is not always the most important factor in the choice of lamps, however. Street lighting mainly uses sodium lighting, as its high energy-efficiency and long lamp life out-weigh its awful orange-coloured light output. Fortunately, most other light sources

above: White walls have a high reflectance; relatively low levels of light can be used to light the walls and throw the spiral topiary into silhouette.

REFLECTANCE OF LANDSCAPE SURFACES		
MATERIAL	**REFLECTANCE (%)**	**LIGHTING LEVEL REQUIRED TO ACHIEVE EQUAL BRIGHTNESS (LUX)**
White paint	75	133
Light stone or brick	50	200
White marble	45	225
Concrete	40	250
Red brick	30	350
Vegetation	25	400
Slate	18	550
Dark stone	18	550
Asphalt	7	1400
Moist soil	7	1400
Grass	6	1666

above right: Types of lamps used in garden lighting. From left: PAR38 tungsten reflector lamp; 12-volt (automotive) tungsten lamp; tungsten 'light bulb'; tungsten halogen lamps in reflector, capsule and linear types; compact fluorescent lamps; metal halide lamps.

aim at a closer approximation to daylight. Metal halide sources and tungsten halogen lamps provide particularly good colour rendering.

Colour temperature

Another measure for lamp types provides a relative indication of the colour of light. This is the colour temperature, which is expressed in degrees Kelvin or K (273K is equal to 0°C/32°F). What might be thought of as warm colours – yellows and oranges – are, in fact, at a lower temperature than the cool blues (see table below). Tungsten halogen and the 3000K metal halide lamps are among the most pleasing to use in garden-lighting design because their fairly white light tends to flatter the natural colours of flowers, foliage and building materials and fits in with our perception of 'natural' colour. Fluorescent lamps are available in a range from warm to cool white for different applications. Warm white is favoured in most gardens because it resembles the colour of tungsten lighting, which has a mellow look. Cool white, on the other hand, tends to look harsh.

Lamp life

Lamp life is another factor to consider, particularly for lighting that is in regular use – for example if it is switched on every night by a timer or photocell. Lamp life is rated in units of 1000 hours and is given by manufacturers as an average lamp life (see table on page 17). Think of 1000 hours as being the equivalent of switching on your garden lighting for three hours every night of the year: a lamp with a life of 1000 hours will, therefore, last roughly a year. Both tungsten and tungsten halogen lamps produce light by incandescence – that is, passing electricity through a filament to heat it until it glows. Other types of 'discharge' lamps produce light by using electricity to strike an arc through a gas-filled tube or envelope in such a way that either the gas or a coating on the inside of the envelope 'fluoresces' or glows. These lamps also use less energy and are becoming increasingly popular for wall lights and lantern fittings. Long-lived, high-intensity discharge lamps, such as the metal halide types, are used for uplighting large trees.

LAMP	COLOUR TEMPERATURE (K)	COLOUR/TONE
Sodium street lighting	1800–2000	Orange/warm
Tungsten	2700	Yellow/warm
Tungsten halogen	2900–3000	White
Metal halide	3000–6000	White or blue/cool
Mercury vapour	3500–4000	Blue/cool

Energy efficiency

Energy efficiency is another advantage of tungsten halogen over tungsten lamps. Not only do tungsten halogen capsule and reflector lamps run on 12 volts – a safe voltage to have outdoors – but they are also very efficient. Use of halogen gas inside the glass capsule around the filament recycles tungsten shed by the filament and enables the lamp to operate at a higher temperature and for longer. This doubles both the lamp life and the light output per watt compared to a typical tungsten lamp. Compact fluorescent lamps typically use about 20 per cent of the power of a tungsten lamp for the same light output. For higher power applications, such as uplighting large trees, a metal halide lamp will typically save more than 85 per cent of the energy of a tungsten lamp or 75 per cent of the energy of a linear halogen floodlight lamp doing the same job.

Choosing a system

Depending on your requirements, each type of commonly used lighting system has its advantages and disadvantages in terms of cost, colour, energy efficiency and flexibility.

Tungsten projector lamps

The mainstay of garden lighting for many years was the PAR type of lamp. PAR stands for Parabolic Aluminized Reflector, and the most common example is the PAR38 lamp, a reflector lamp, 120mm (4³/₄in) in diameter, usually with an Edison screw base or cap and intended for use in a mains voltage (also known as line voltage) spike- or wall-mount holder. This type of lamp has always been relatively inexpensive and widely available, and requires little specialist knowledge to use and create a simple lighting scheme. One drawback is that it is mainly available in higher wattages, from 60 watts upwards, but it is a popular lamp for the general uplighting of trees. In this role, a spot or flood beam is suitable for lighting columnar and spreading trees. It is

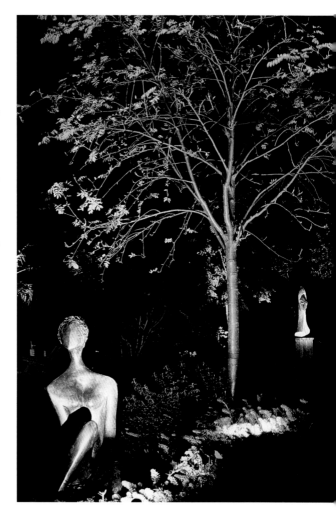

available with colour coatings, usually green, red, yellow and blue, but this kind of colour treatment of natural subjects in a garden often produces a garish effect, which overwhelms rather than reinforces the natural appearance of foliage, stone and timber. A green lamp tends to make a specimen tree or shrub look like a plastic Christmas tree.

above: The bluish hue of the tree is a result of uplighting with a mercury vapour lamp; this contrasts with the colour achieved by illuminating the statues with white light from tungsten halogen lamps.

LAMP	TYPICAL LIFE (hours)
Tungsten	1000
Tungsten halogen capsule	2000
Tungsten halogen spotlight	3000–4000
Compact fluorescent	5000–10,000
Metal halide	up to 10,000

COMPARISONS OF LAMPS WITHOUT REFLECTOR OR FOR USE WITH EXTERNAL REFLECTOR

LAMP SHAPE	LAMP TYPE	LAMP LIFE (hours)	EFFICIENCY (Lumens per watt)	COLOUR TEMPERATURE (K)	FEATURES AND APPLICATIONS IN EXTERIOR LIGHTING
	tungsten bulb	1000	9–13	2700	**Pros:** Low cost, familiar product provides warm lighting in wall lights **Cons:** Poor energy efficiency and lamp life
	tungsten halogen capsule	2000	15–25	2900	**Pros:** Twice the lamp life and energy efficiency of a tungsten bulb, white light, miniature size **Cons:** 12 volt – needs transformer
	tungsten halogen linear	2000	15–20	3000	**Pros:** High power white light for floodlighting **Cons:** High power consumption; unsuitable for focused lighting
	compact fluorescent	5000–10000	50–65	2900–4000	**Pros:** Long lamp life, good energy efficiency, warm and cool colours **Cons:** Coiled tubes not attractive but new 'bulb' shapes appearing
	metal halide (ceramic)	9000	80–100	3000–4200	**Pros:** High energy efficiency, long life, choice of white and cool light good for focused lighting of trees, etc **Cons:** Luminaires fairly expensive
	mercury vapour	12000–24000	19–63	3500–4000	**Pros:** Good energy efficiency and life **Cons:** Luminaires relatively expensive, cool bluish light not suitable for many applications
	high pressure sodium	14000–55000	66–140	2000	**Pros:** Exceptional lamp life and high energy efficiency, popular for street and commercial lighting **Cons:** Orange colour rendering
	low pressure sodium	16000	100–198	1800	**Pros:** Exceptional energy efficiency and long life popular for street lighting **Cons:** Orange colour rendering

Tungsten halogen dichroic lamps

Creative garden lighting has recently come to be dominated by the MR16 low-voltage halogen lamp. This 50mm (2in) diameter lamp features a miniature halogen capsule lamp mounted in a multi-mirror reflector to provide a controlled beam of light with little peripheral light spill. These lamps run on 12 volts, so, although transformers must be installed, they permit flexible wiring configurations and easy adjustment.

The MR16 is twice as energy efficient as the PAR38 tungsten lamp. The 'dichroic' reflector reflects all the light forward, while allowing much of the heat to dissipate through the rear of the lamp – that is, it projects much less heat towards your planting or down on to the dining table. MR16 lamps are available in wattages from 10 to 75 and beam angles from 7 to 60 degrees, giving much more choice in accurately and precisely lighting subjects without glare. The wide range of lamp choice is reinforced by its small size: it is less than half the diameter of a PAR38 lamp and about 10 per cent of its overall size. Using MR16 lamps means that luminaires can be much smaller and yet produce more light than old-fashioned tungsten fittings, allowing much greater flexibility in their use.

Positioning

When you are choosing subjects to light in a garden, it does not necessarily follow that a higher wattage lamp will produce a brighter effect. Spotlighting by using a narrow-beam halogen lamp will produce a more intense circle of light than a wider beam of the same wattage, and a narrow-beam reflector more tightly focuses the light emitted by the halogen capsule into a higher concentration in a smaller circle. This not only makes best use of the wattage capability of a lamp but also serves to make the subject that is being lit more prominent than the other objects around it. A narrow-beam, 20-watt lamp can provide a much higher light level in the centre of its beam than a wide-angle, 50-watt lamp in which the light is not focused so tightly. Perhaps surprisingly, therefore, higher-wattage, wide-beam lamps are often used for the general illumination of mature shrub borders and spreading trees, while lower-wattage, narrower-beam lamps are used to accent individual features. The table below summarizes and compares the characteristics of tungsten PAR38 and tungsten halogen reflector lamps and details the advantages and disadvantages of using each. There is also an indication of the ways in which each lamp can be used in the garden.

above: An MR16 halogen reflector lamp is about one-tenth of the overall size of a PAR38 tungsten projector lamp, but provides the same light output.

COMPARISONS OF REFLECTOR LAMPS

LAMP SHAPE	LAMP TYPE	LAMP LIFE (hours)	EFFICIENCY (Candelas per watt)	COLOUR TEMPERATURE (K)	FEATURES AND APPLICATIONS IN EXTERIOR LIGHTING
	tungsten PAR38 projector (flood 30° beam)	1000–2000	20–24	2700	**Pros:** Low cost, familiar product provides warm lighting **Cons:** Poor energy efficiency and lamp life; limited range of beam angles and wattages; large size
	tungsten halogen reflector (flood 36° beam)	3000–5000	50	3000	**Pros:** White light, small size, twice lamp life and energy efficiency of tungsten projector lamp, wide choice of beam angles and wattages (10–75w) **Cons:** 12 volts – needs transformer

Types of garden lighting

above: Bollard lights illuminate this steep flight of steps to provide safe access; mains-voltage bollard lights provide high light output which is often more functional than decorative.

Designing a garden lighting scheme is not just a question of selecting from among the range of wall-mounted, recessed or spike-mount lights. It is also important to distinguish between the ways in which power can be introduced into the garden and to match the different types of light source that are available to the appropriate features. Steps, for example, will be lit in a quite different way from a specimen tree, or the area around a barbecue.

Types of light fitting

One of the problems with introducing lighting into the garden is that the names given to light fittings are either confusing or apparently inappropriate or both. Some names simply express what a light fitting does – floodlights and spotlights, for example. Other names, however, may describe the ways in which the fitting is mounted (wall lights and steplights), its direction (uplights and downlights), its power source (solar lights and low-voltage lights) or its function (security lights). Other names have a historical, rather than a functional, resonance – the term bulkhead lights derive from the original maritime usage, coachlamps date from the days of horse power, and lanterns remind us of the time when this was a convenient way of carrying a candle or oil lamp.

Mains-voltage lighting

Until a couple of decades ago, nearly all lighting was mains (line) voltage – that is, it was powered from the utility supply voltage, usually somewhere between 110 and 240 volts and 'harmonized' in Europe at a nominal 230 volts. The light sources that were used in garden lighting were predominantly the tungsten 'light bulb' for wall lights, lanterns of various types and PAR projector lamps, mainly the PAR38 lamp rated at 60–120 watts. These sources still survive in residential use, partly because of their low initial cost and partly because energy-saving lighting and lighting design in the home are far from widely employed or understood among non-specialists.

Of the more modern mains-voltage light sources, compact fluorescent lamps are gradually taking over from tungsten in exterior wall lights and lanterns, while metal halide high-pressure discharge lighting is becoming the main way of uplighting large trees and architectural features. Metal halide floodlights and uplights provide a range of energy-efficient lighting power beyond that which can be handled by 12-volt equipment.

Low-voltage lighting

In low-voltage systems mains voltage is reduced through a transformer to 12 or 24 volts, which is a safe level of voltage, incapable of giving a fatal shock. This means that flexible cables can be used around the garden rather than the fixed cabling required for mains-voltage systems. In Europe these low voltages are described as 'safety extra-low voltage'.

The use of low-voltage lighting in gardens originates from two sources. Firstly, low-voltage halogen lighting, originally developed for lighting shop displays and works of art in museums and art galleries. This was recognized as the means by which theatre lighting techniques could be miniaturized and transferred to landscape lighting. This was adopted mainly for commercial and public applications initially, but

below: A low-voltage spreadlight provides a pool of light around a path or low planting, while hiding the light source under the 'hat' on top.

it is now increasingly used for private gardens. Secondly, automotive tungsten lamps were adopted as a simple means of providing low-power illumination in the garden from a transformer in the house, avoiding the need to lay protected mains-voltage cabling outside.

Garden-lighting kits

The market for garden-lighting kits developed rapidly as fittings made from inexpensive materials, especially plastic, made garden lighting more affordable. Some manufacturers built transformers into weatherproof boxes and adopted thicker low-voltage cabling so that lighting could be extended farther out into the garden, and they used metal fittings that could withstand the heat of a higher-power lamp. More recently, the original

tungsten lamps have been increasingly replaced by more efficient, longer-life, halogen reflector lamps in spotlights and halogen capsule lamps in step and path lights.

Commercial landscape lighting aside, the garden-lighting market has tended to polarize into 'professional' garden lighting, principally distributed by lighting or landscape specialists offering related design services, and the retail sector, offering a combination of inexpensive tungsten PAR38 mains-voltage lighting and plastic low-voltage garden-lighting kits.

Most garden retail outlets offer at least one range of garden-lighting kits. It will usually include light fittings made from plastic to reduce cost and for easy assembly, requiring few tools and little electrical knowledge. The lights are attached to a ribbed cable by clamp-on

LOW-VOLTAGE LIGHTING

Where lights are to be used adjacent to or near the house, the transformer can be located inside the house and either plugged or wired into a socket or other electrical outlet. The low-voltage cable can be taken outside through a hole drilled in the wall and the luminaires connected to it. The cable should be protected in conduit under paving or through gravel or hard-core layers, but can otherwise be run on the surface of the soil, hidden by low planting or a layer of mulch.

Low-power plastic luminaires may clip on to the cable, whereas higher-power metal luminaires will usually require a cable joint using screw-nuts, crimp connectors or terminal blocks. Transformers meant for 'interior use only' should never be used outside. Low-power, low-voltage lights may be sited only up to 20m (60ft) from the transformer. For lights farther from the house or of 20 watts or more in power, install exterior transformers and mains-voltage exterior cabling to the transformer locations.

switch

transformer

low voltage cable protected by plastic conduit

cable laid on surface of soil and covered with bark or wood chip mulch left: A typical low-voltage kit for pathlighting, consisting of a transformer for interior installation, cable and plastic luminaires with low-voltage lamps.

below: This plastic bollard light is from a low-voltage kit powered from an interior transformer. It illuminates a small area of paving or low planting. As the lamp is low power, glare from the unshielded light source is unlikely to be a problem.

connectors, in which sharp contacts pierce the insulation to make contact with the conducting wires inside. The low-voltage cable connects easily to a transformer, which is usually designed for interior use and is fitted with a plug suitable for socket outlets in the country of use.

The limiting factor is the material from which the lights are made, which is usually moulded plastic. Most such plastics deform in close proximity to heat, so the lamps used tend to be relatively low power, often 10 watts or below. Although some are available as spotlights, the majority are designed as miniature lanterns, globes or as a 'pagoda' design, and their main role tends to be marking out a path or perhaps providing low-level lighting by steps or a patio. The low power limits their usefulness in larger gardens or for lighting anything but smaller garden features. They are, however, a means of providing safe lighting where the installation of mains-voltage cables along walls or structures or in trenches at a safe depth would be impossible or, at least, too disruptive to be practical.

Kits are also often a useful way to experiment, which may later lead a

home-owner to consider a scheme using higher-power metal products for larger features or areas in the garden.

It is important to check whether the transformer is suitable for use indoors, in the house, garage or an outbuilding only. If a transformer

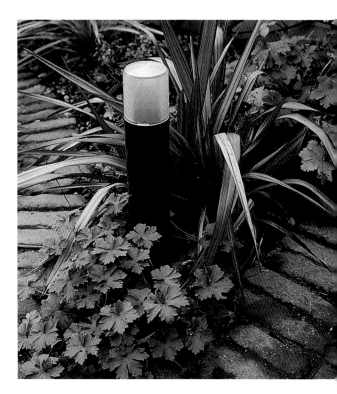

suitable for exterior use is provided and that is where you wish to locate it, you should budget for the services of a professional electrician to install it.

Solar lighting

The idea behind self-contained solar-powered lighting products is the same as for garden-lighting kits: the provision of low-power garden lighting without the need for mains-voltage cabling. Common forms include miniature lanterns or pagodas. A small photovoltaic solar panel on top of each luminaire charges an internal battery by day, and the light is switched on by a photocell at dusk. Some models include a movement detector to switch on the light when someone passes by. The light sources are usually fairly low power to strike a balance between brightness and battery life. How long they remain lit obviously depends on the power of the light source, the size of the battery and the extent of recharge provided by the duration and intensity of sunlight. Brighter models may boast five hours of lighting after recharge in bright sunlight, whereas other

below: This small solar light is designed to mark the route along the edge of a path rather than light a particular area. The compact design features a small solar-electric cell which provides limited recharge capacity for a battery and a low-wattage lamp.

models are lower powered and are intended mainly for marking the way along a path.

The battery, which is charged and recharged on a regular cycle, will need to be replaced at regular intervals. Nickel cadmium batteries usually need to be replaced after about 500 cycles, which equates to about 18 months of daily use. A more professional standard of lighting and electrical power can be achieved using a system of batteries charged from solar panels on the roof of an outbuilding, but this type of specialist installation is outside the scope of this book.

Directional lighting

Landscape lighting professionals use projector types of lamp, particularly low-voltage halogen dichroic lamps but also other types of halogen lamps and some high-pressure discharge types,

left: Regularly spaced spreadlights provide effective pathlighting without detracting from other illuminated garden features along the route.

such as metal halide lamps, to create directional lighting. The range of lamp beams will range from 'very narrow spot' to 'very wide flood'. It can be a spike-mount spotlight, which performs the function of uplighting, or wall-mounted, which performs the function of downlighting. The terms uplight, or uplighter, and downlight, or downlighter, also describe products that perform those lighting functions. The effects for which they are used are described in 'Garden-lighting effects'.

Path- and steplights

Paths and steps are often lit with spotlights mounted on structures or trees. Where there are no such lighting positions, specific lights need to be incorporated in the lighting design to fulfil this function. Where there are flanking walls, the use of discreet surface or recessed steplights

left: Spike-mount tungsten halogen spotlights are versatile tools for lighting a range of subjects. This type of copper spotlight weathers to an attractive mottled brown finish and can utilize a variety of lamp wattage and beam angles to produce different effects.

above: Area lighting of steps is effective for access purposes, but produces a bland effect devoid of features or emphasis.

or bricklights provide localized lighting. In the absence of walls, the choice is often between spreadlights (lights on a stick) and bollard lights (lights in a stick). These products may also be used to provide low-level lighting around patios and drives, while area lighting products (see below) may also be used if higher light levels are required.

Area lighting
Providing lighting across a horizontal area is usually the preserve of mains-voltage lighting, largely because a wide choice of luminaires is available in finishes to suit all architectural styles. Although the mounting position may vary from wall mount or pillar top to column or pole mount, such lights rely mainly on 'diffusion' light sources to spread light around them, although some models have internal reflectors to maximize the outward spread of light.

Floodlights
Floodlighting aims to reproduce the all-embracing illumination of the sun. It is seen at its most extreme form in sports stadia, where the aim is to allow sport to be conducted in conditions as near to daylight as possible. This is not what garden lighting is about.

There are some requirements for high levels of lighting in gardens for which floodlighting may be appropriate – a tennis or badminton court or a croquet lawn, perhaps, or an area where horses are kept in the country. In suburban gardens the need is more usually for lighting the children's football game on the lawn or downlighting paved areas for parties.

Security lights
Floodlighting is often thought of as the only means of security lighting, but there are alternatives (see pages 38–9). The term 'security light' is usually associated with an individual floodlight or wall-mounted luminaire with a built-in movement detector that switches on the light when an intruder comes within the zone of coverage. The use of built-in detectors is often a cost consideration rather than one aimed at providing optimum performance: such luminaires are often less expensive but easier to fit on a do-it-yourself basis.

Linear lighting
Lighting a structure or a linear feature has, until recently, been largely achieved by projecting a beam of light towards it or by placing luminaires to diffuse light on to it. In recent years trends in

lighting technology have conspired to produce a more novel approach called 'outlining', either using the light sources themselves to emphasize the linearity or using a hidden array of light to provide a linear effect. Each type of product tends to have its own associated lighting effect, so these are dealt with here, rather than in later chapters. Some types of lighting, such as cold cathode and neon lighting, are used by professionals; they require customized configuration and would be too complex to install in most gardens. The principal products used in garden lighting are string lighting, tape lighting and fibre-optic lighting.

Stringlighting

Stringlighting is most familiar as the small lights strung on Christmas trees. Christmas lighting products described as being suitable for exterior use are not designed for long-term outdoor applications. They have a short lamp life and the transformers supplied are often not rated for exterior installation. They rely on the transformer being located in the house or an outbuilding, with the lighting cable being led out

through a window or vent. If a transformer suitable for exterior use is provided and that is where you wish to locate it, you should employ a professional electrician to install it.

A variation on this theme is rope light where a lighting string is threaded through a clear, flexible polythene hose. The lamp life is relatively short but this is a popular form of inexpensive outdoor lighting for parties and other festive occasions. Rope light is usually a 240-volt product, so proper installation outside is essential, and use near water is not advised. Christmas-tree lighting is usually a zig-zag effect of lighting strung around the tree, while rope lighting is often wound around the trunks of palm trees in Middle Eastern countries.

above: Lighting emphasizes hard landscaping, which can produce an effect described as 'stark' or 'minimalist' depending on your point of view.

left: Ornamental lanterns can be chosen for decorative purposes, as well as for garden illumination.

Long-life stringlighting

If you have a bigger budget you may consider a more permanent display. Commercial string lighting uses Xenon lamps, which last up to 20,000 hours. This means that you can put the stringlights up in a tree and forget about them for several years, just switching them on when you want to instead of getting the ladder out to put temporary ones up every time Christmas or a party comes around.

The most stylish way of using stringlighting in anything other than a dense conifer is to achieve an outlining effect on a tree with a less dense canopy. Fix the string lighting up the trunk and along the branches so that the finished effect is of lines of lights tracing out the structure of the tree. Tie the string into place with degradable garden twine, which will break if the tree outgrows its grip; do not use plastic fixings, such as plastic electrical ties or metal wire, because they could throttle a growing branch. If cable clips need to be fixed to the trunk, use stainless-steel pins; never use brass screws, as they poison many types of tree. The lamps are typically under 10mm (under $\frac{1}{2}$in) in diameter and are rated at around 1 watt each. Commercial Christmas tree lighting for public displays often uses higher-power lighting in globes.

Tape lighting

Outlining is not used only for trees. In many countries it is used widely as a means of lighting a gazebo or pergola, partly to outline the structure and partly to provide some subtle lighting for the area within. Some people regard this type of lighting as too much like that found in a theme park or pleasure beach for a domestic lighting role model, but in a modern garden used as

right: Linear lighting outlines the structure of the gazebo and provides some ambient lighting within.

an outdoor room such lighting can provide excitement all year round.

Outlining has further developed to provide linear lighting in more easily concealed strip format. The conductors are contained within a flat, insulated plastic tape, which can be fixed to flat surfaces, or in miniature versions where the light string is concealed within plastic or metal strip for fixing under steps, for example. Light-emitting diodes with a long lamp life are currently being tipped as a successor for existing exterior light sources, and they may feature in further developments of tape light, but at present they have not achieved widespread commercial use.

Fibre-optic lighting

Fibre-optic lighting is often described as a new technology, but it has been around for more than 20 years. It is available in two forms: side-emitting and end-emitting. Side-emitting fibre is used for outlining. Optical glass fibres are bundled together in a clear sleeve, so the light is projected along the entire length of the cable from a remotely mounted control box containing a focused lamp assembly

designed for the purpose. In end-emitting fibre-optic lighting the glass fibres are encased in a black sheath and the light is emitted at the end of each 'tail' running from the control box. It is focused through a glass lens, either to provide a pinpoint of light or to project a beam of light on a subject.

While fibre-optic lighting is still relatively expensive for widespread use in domestic gardens, its appeal lies in the fact that the fibre-optic cable carries no heat or electricity, which makes it very useful in water features. Only one lamp needs to be replaced for a whole lighting array, and a colour-wheel option means that changing colour effects can be achieved fairly simply, if required. Popular applications include outlining around the edge of a pool and accent lighting within complex water features, where electric lighting would be difficult to install or it would be difficult to change lamps. However, fibre-optic lighting is not a general-purpose product. Each installation needs to be precisely engineered, and ducting into the features in which it is installed can be equally complex, so it is essential to get specialist help.

above: Stringlighting adds an unusual touch to this line of espalier apple trees in winter.

The purpose
of lighting

above: Underwater lighting of the wall fountain is framed by the lighting of the large urns, drawing the eye downward in this courtyard and away from the city lights outside. Downlighting the paved area adds foreground illumination for al fresco dining.

When you start to think about designing a lighting system for your garden you must first understand the roles lighting will play in the use and enjoyment of each part of your exterior space. The way you will use the garden and your choice of lighting will have fundamental implications for the planning of the system, including the sources of power, the number of circuits and the position and type of controls.

Choosing a type of lighting

Begin by dividing the garden into areas that you know will be used differently, and draw up a table to facilitate detailed planning later. Then, within each area, look at your lighting needs.

Identifying your lighting needs

Before you can draw up a plan of a lighting scheme, decide what you will use the lighting for. There are five main types of lighting.

• **Ornamental lighting** is used when garden features are lit for visual appeal.

• **Amenity lighting** is introduced for safety and practical purposes – for example, on a patio to light a dining area or on a drive to help move shopping or children from the car.

• **Task lighting** makes it possible to carry out specific jobs, such as cooking on a barbecue or fetching objects from an outbuilding.

• **Access lighting** permits safe movement around the garden by lighting paths, steps, doors and water.

• **Security lighting** deters intruders, creates an illusion of occupation and reassures home-owners.

There may be some overlap. You may write 'ornamental/access' for an area in which ornamental lighting to enhance an area must be complemented by safe path illumination – for example, in a woodland walk. In the same way, 'access/ornamental' would be appropriate for where good pathlighting is required between the house and a swimming pool but there are also trees and shrubs that should be lit to provide interest on the way. Some specific types of lighting may apply to certain areas – floodlighting for the tennis court or croquet pitch and underwater lighting in the swimming pool, for example, but, at this stage, concentrate on summarizing as simply as possible what you believe each area requires and the order of priority between the functions. Your table will develop further as you choose the lighting effects and start the detailed planning of the installation.

Ornamental lighting

A good start in developing a garden lighting plan is to focus first on the ornamental lighting effects you want to achieve and the areas of the garden in which they will be applied, as we usually expect that lighting in all or most areas will have at least some ornamental value. Ask yourself the following questions:

• Do I want to see this lighting only when I am in the garden?

• Do I want to see this lighting only when I am in the house and, if so, from which rooms?

• Do I want to see this lighting from both inside and outside and, if so, from which rooms or areas?

• Will I see this lighting only from a selected viewpoint inside the house or outside the house?

• Should the ornamental lighting primarily provide a welcoming view of the house?

This may all seem obvious, but some home-owners see lighting only as a means of prolonging their enjoyment of warm evenings in the garden, while those who live in less temperate areas will need the illuminated view from the

below: Uplighting from below galvanized mesh reflects from mirrors and galvanized planters to provide a subtle setting for architectural planting.

Area of garden	Type of lighting
Ornamental garden areas (water features, trees, etc)	Ornamental lighting
Drives	Amenity and security lighting
Paths and steps	Access and ornamental lighting
Entrances	Access, ornamental and security lighting
Sitting and eating areas	Amenity and task lighting
Activity areas (swimming pools, tennis courts, etc)	Access lighting and other lighting specific to the function

house. Do not make the mistake of thinking that ornamental lighting is only about creating dramatic focal points. Drama can be created when and where you want, but the aim of ornamental lighting is usually to create an atmosphere and a balanced view of the garden that is easy on the eye.

Identifying viewpoints

The next requirement is to establish the viewpoints from which these areas of the garden and the features within them may be seen. This will determine the complexity of your lighting system.

In a small garden the answer may be a simple one. If the reception rooms face on to the rear garden so that all or most of it can be seen from all of the rear windows, for example, and the patio is immediately adjacent to the house, a simple, single-circuit ornamental lighting system is likely to be adequate. All the ornamental lighting will be switched on together, and all the lighting will be appreciated from any viewpoint on the patio or in the house.

You are, however, also likely to have some lights on the wall of the house to

below: Lighting a view out of the window is the main requirement when cooler or wetter evenings are more common.

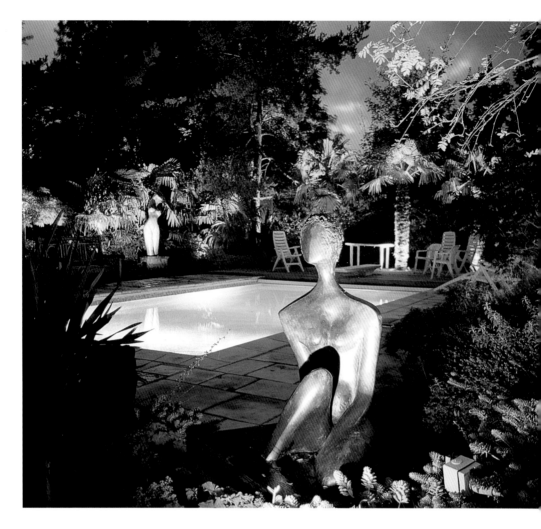

provide lighting for other purposes, such as lighting the patio area for dining or barbecuing or perhaps for safe passage to a side gate, shed or garage. If such wiring is possible, it will be useful to have separate switches for the wall lights and the garden lighting on the same switch panel, conveniently located by one or more of the doors or windows facing the rear garden.

In larger gardens or in properties with a more complex building or garden layout, more thought will be needed. Establishing viewpoints for individual areas or features from different rooms or outside seating areas will help to determine the lighting design and how the system should be wired and controlled. If different areas of the garden are visible only from certain viewpoints, there may be little point in switching on all the lighting in the

whole garden if only one area can be seen from the room most usually in use. Even if you wish to have a central switch panel for all the lighting – in a central hallway, for example – you may still wish to control the lighting in separate areas in different ways.

Amenity lighting

Once you have developed your ideas for ornamental lighting, you should think about potential requirements in other areas, such as providing lighting for practical activities and ensuring that the lighting also means a safe garden and a secure home. General lighting that enables you to perform a range of functions, from inserting a key in a lock, through seeing the meal you are about to enjoy, to avoiding treading on children's toys that have been left on the terrace, is known as amenity

above: Ornamental lighting of statues, trees and shrubs provides a continuous vista around the pool, while underwater lighting diffuses to provide general illumination of the poolside.

tungsten 'bulbs', compact fluorescent lamps or, perhaps, halogen capsule lamps for small areas. These will usually be fixed on the face of the building, mounted on top of a garden wall or gate pillar or supported on a post or column of one size or another. They diffuse lighting all around and downwards and many designs will be partially shielded to avoid projecting light upwards to pollute the night sky or to annoy your neighbours.

The style chosen should reflect the architectural character of your house and your own taste. A general-purpose lampholder (bayonet cap or Edison screw) gives flexibility in the choice of lamp type and wattage. These choices are often a compromise between the maximum heat permissible within the luminaire, the light output required, the appearance of the lamp and the colour of the light emitted.

Floodlighting is rarely satisfactory for amenity lighting in private gardens, unless it is on a separate circuit that can be switched on only when higher-power lighting is required, such as retrieving objects from an area or providing adequate lighting when there are a lot of people at a function. Even then, the power should be limited to 150 watts per floodlight because above this level glare starts to become a significant problem. Higher-power floodlighting should be reserved for sporting activity and security lighting, and even then it should be installed to be effective only within the property boundary.

above: Uplighting reflects from the white walls to provide illumination within a small courtyard garden, helping to distract the eye from the surrounding buildings.

lighting. Normally, this requirement is fulfilled by area lighting, although occasionally luminaires placed for decorative effect also fulfil the role of amenity lighting. Recessed downlights under a porch canopy, for example, perform the decorative function of illuminating a front door and creating a welcome focal point for anyone approaching the house, but they also provide enough light to light your way through the door and safely over the step. Downlighting from a pergola or from under the eaves of a house are ways of using directional lighting for a patio.

Area lighting

Where there is no convenient structure for an overhead lighting platform, most amenity lighting is provided by general area lighting – luminaires with

Task lighting

Daylight is normally associated with carrying out tasks outside, whether it be gardening or chopping logs, but there are tasks performed during leisure time for which lighting is essential, eg carrying dishes from the kitchen to the patio table. While you are introducing cables to your garden and home to provide ornamental and amenity lighting, make sure you give yourself flexibility and choice so that you can use the lighting to its fullest extent.

left: Uplighting of the house façade coupled with downlighting of the decking and linear lighting of the steps produces an impression which is both ornamental and practical.

If you include a separate, weatherproof switch for task lighting around or above the barbecue, you will be able to switch it off when the cooking is finished so that you are not viewing the smoking remains while you dine. Equally, you do not really want the door of the shed lit all evening for the sake of putting things away at the end of the evening. Defining these tasks at an early part of planning stage means you can put convenient switches in the right places, probably at little extra cost.

Access lighting

Access lighting is concerned mainly with lighting routes into and around the garden and house. The boundary between access and amenity lighting gets blurred the closer we get to the house or outbuildings, where lighting is associated with fetching and carrying as opposed to just walking.

Access lighting can be achieved by a variety of techniques. Its purpose is primarily safety, yet it can also be seen partly as amenity lighting and partly as ornamental lighting. The primary need

below: Uplighting and spreadlighting at intervals along this 120m (400ft) driveway lined with *Cupressus Leylandii* conspire to provide ornamental access lighting.

SAFETY CHECKLIST	
POTENTIAL DANGER	**POSITION OF HAZARD**
Change of level	Steps, ramps, unfenced decks or patios
Change of direction	Intersections or bends in paths
Entrances	Doors, gateways
Pedestrian routes	Drives, paths
Paths near or over water	Bridges, stepping stones, pool edges or banks
Open areas used to travel around the garden	Terraces, patios, lawns, paved or gravelled areas
Obstacles	Trees near paths, overhanging beams or branches
Specific dangers	Barbecues, play equipment, moving machinery

is to ensure that the route is safe. It can be used to highlight waymarks that you need to see – the gate tucked into a hedge will not announce itself unless you have bothered to signal its presence with lighting. Access lighting should be used to lihgt the driveway to the front door also to highlight the door number and name. The approach should be well lit so that the visitor has a welcoming focus for direction.

Finally, don't treat the lighting of paths and drives purely as a utilitarian exercise; consider ways to light planting and garden features along the way to act as signposts to guide the visitor safely and attractively. For example, make the lighting entertaining by 'moonlighting' down from trees to provide natural lighting for a driveway. The illusion of moonlight filtering down through branches and leaves to create dappled patterns of light and shadow on the area below is more aesthetically pleasing than installing bollard lights or 'street' lights along the verge.

Lighting for safety

Nowhere is good lighting practice more important than in lighting for access and safety. Making someone feel wholly disoriented when they reach the top of a flight of stairs by confronting them with the beam of a badly placed spotlight is as dangerous as failing to light the steps at all. Lighting for safety

right: The underwater lighting in the pool defines the area of hazard for anyone walking around this area of the garden.

can be achieved by a variety of techniques. For example, pathlighting can be achieved by lighting provided for ornamental value (moonlighting from a tree), by specific access lighting (spreadlights in adjacent planting), by area lighting on the walls of the house or as the result of a task-lighting requirement (fetching barbecue fuel from the shed).

A safety audit

Not all of the safety concerns listed above will arise in every garden, as garden designs are so individual and the way people use their garden at night varies widely. In a garden with no routes to the end of the garden for access to rear gates or sheds, it will not be necessary to light the lawn as if it were a path, but it would be possible to illuminate it as a 'horizontal feature'.

It is worth considering the safety aspects from two viewpoints: that of the homeowner who knows the layout and possible hazards in the garden, and that of a visitor who is unaware of any danger lurking in the dark. For the home-owner, good area lighting should have eliminated places where you might

above: Recessed uplights with low-wattage lamps are a subtle way of marking out the pool edge for safety.

SAFETY AROUND WATER

There are always areas in gardens where safety lighting is needed, but it can be achieved in a decorative manner. In modern gardens especially, because contemporary design seems to avoid using conventional balustrades or fencing at the edge of levels, it is particularly associated with decking and water (although not necessarily together). Although underwater lighting is not as common as you might expect, it is particularly important to mark the edge of a patio or deck so that an inattentive person does not take an unplanned swim. The same is true of stepping stones and plank bridges over water. Recessed lights set into the walls of a swimming pool address this danger during night-time parties around the pools and also allow others to see a swimmer in difficulty.

above: Uplighting the trees and shrubs around a pool provides focal points and gives form to the area.

system triggered by passive infra-red detectors that sense body heat and switch on the lighting when the heat source moves towards the building. The system is often zoned, so that floodlighting on different parts of the house can be monitored or switched on or off manually if required.

The ability to switch off such lighting is essential if you are going to invest in a subtle garden-lighting system and wish to avoid being blinded by floodlights every time you reach for a glass of wine. Many security experts now believe that this form of lighting is no deterrent to the determined professional thief but accept that it has a value in deterring casual would-be intruders and in providing home-owners with some reassurance that they have adopted the 'appropriate measures' suggested by insurance companies.

The value of such protection is often reduced because the detectors are mounted on the house and so are activated only after the intruder has entered the property. This can be resolved by locating remote detectors and beam fences, but this strays into the world of the professional security specialist. Although technology has improved to avoid 'false triggering', wind-blown branches and wildlife still cause lights to come on. This can be reduced by the choice of quality equipment and careful positioning of detectors, but false triggering will always be an occasional feature of such systems and can be a cause of anxiety about whether someone is lurking outside.

trip on an unseen obstacle, and task lighting will have reduced the risk of burns resulting from cooking on the barbecue in lower light levels. Beyond the specific lighting that is provided, the home-owner's knowledge of their own property provides them with added protection, or at least foreknowledge of hazards. For the visitor, good path- and steplighting should illuminate hazards in unfamiliar territory. These might include places where the ground falls away at one side or where it would be easy to collide with a tree immediately to the side of the path, and entrances should be lit in a welcoming manner to show the most direct and safe way.

Security lighting

For many people security lighting is about deterrence, and the common solution, especially by security companies, is to install a floodlighting

Creating the illusion of occupation

Some home-owners prefer to use lighting to create the illusion that someone is in. This usually involves lighting that comes on automatically at dusk and either stays on all night or is switched off by a timer when residents usually go to bed. This regular pattern of lighting makes it look as if the house is always occupied, especially if selected interior lighting operates in the same way. It is also possible for such lighting to switch on again automatically if movement is detected after the timer has switched off the lighting or to have panic buttons on the upper floors so that occupants can switch on the lighting if disturbing noises are heard. This form of security lighting often incorporates wall lights on the house, supplemented by lighting drives and gateways, but the garden's ornamental lighting circuits can also be incorporated into the scheme.

Reassuring the homeowner

Security lighting makes the homeowner feel safer. This is partly based on the idea that good lighting is one of the best deterrents against intruders and partly on the belief that illuminated grounds offer a wider area of deterrence than an illuminated building. Bear in mind, however, that over-ostentatious front-garden lighting may draw your property to the attention of criminals.

One application of ornamental lighting becoming more common, especially in connection with crimes

such as mugging, is lighting shrub borders; this offers reassurance that muggers are not hiding in wait when you return home from an evening out. At their most sophisticated, such schemes can extend to a lighting system that can be switched on from a remote control unit that also opens the gates and garage doors from inside the car.

above left: A twin PAR38 light with an integral passive infra-red movement detector is a cheap but unattractive form of security lighting.

below: Patio spotlights can be timer-operated to provide an illusion of occupation when no-one is at home.

Garden-
lighting effects

above: Light beams create a fascinating interplay of illuminated foliage, shadow and silhouette within this area of strong architectural planting.

Having identified the areas in the garden that need lighting and the type of lighting that is required within them, it is time to turn to the different effects that can be achieved. A fine statue, positioned as a focal point at the end of a shrub border, will be lit in quite a different way from the interesting texture revealed on a house wall. Achieving these distinctive effects will require the use of the full range of lighting methods, which range from the comparatively straightforward techniques of up- and downlighting to the more subtle results that can be achieved by grazing, moonlighting and accent lighting.

frosted lenses are often used for diffused lighting around patios. For downlighting from pergolas, 20- or 35-watt halogen lamps are usually used, while downlighting from trees or under eaves will require 50-watt lamps only for the brightest applications.

left: Downlighting highlights the shape of topiary which would otherwise be hidden in shadow by uplighting from below.

Uplighting

Lighting from below produces an effect that demands attention because it reverses the effect of daylight. The luminaire should be aimed away from the viewpoint or shielded from view so that the beauty of the illuminated object can be appreciated without glare or the distraction of seeing where the lighting originates **(2)**. Where there are multiple viewpoints, external glare shields or internal glare louvres help to achieve the required effect while reducing the glare in several directions.

below: Two metal halide recessed uplights punch light up through the structure of this Cedar of Lebanon. Ground mist reveals the light beams.

Downlighting

Lighting in a downward direction from a structure to provide a pool of light on a surface or feature below can provide general illumination for safety, security and appearance, as well as a contrast to the uplighting of other features. Possibilities include downlighting from a pergola beam onto a dining table or path below, downward grazing and wall washing from under eaves and spotlighting downwards on to statues and other features **(1)**. Downlighting is a useful way to illuminate flowering plants because flowers tend to face upwards rather than downwards; pergola-, wall- and tree-mounted luminaires can be used for this purpose.

Downlighting generally uses lower-power lamps than uplighting because the applications tend to involve lighting downwards toward the eye. Low-power lamps with glare shields and internal glare louvres are widely used, while

Uplighting is obviously the most common garden-lighting technique because ground-mounting is almost universally possible, whereas wall and overhead lighting platforms are not always available. Recessed uplights are recommended in flat areas where a spike-mount light would be visually intrusive, a maintenance problem – mowing a lawn, for example – or a trip hazard – in paving on a terrace or porch. In other instances, spike-mount uplights or spotlights are preferred because they are cheaper than recessed units and are more easily moved or adjusted to suit plant growth or seasonal changes.

Uplighting can produce a variety of effects, including accent lighting, washing and grazing. It is used where special emphasis on a feature, such as a tree, statue, house façade or wall, is required, but is also ideal for 'infill' lighting of shrub borders to provide a visual link between individually illuminated features. Although we think of uplighting as a ground-based function, it can of course be achieved by spotlights mounted on walls, structures and branches and by underwater lights below the surface.

right: Uplighting adjacent shrubs and small trees places the illuminated statue in context with its surroundings.

bottom: Grazing light up the brick wall emphasises its texture, particularly in contrast with the adjacent rendered walls.

1

Grazing

Where texture is an obvious aspect of a feature or surface, lighting at an acute angle from a position near the surface will emphasize it by casting strong shadow **(1)**. The light is 'grazing' the surface (although it is also sometimes called 'texturing') as well as emphasizing its colour. An uplight placed close to the trunk of a tree will emphasize colour, texture and pattern in the bark, while the same uplight placed close to a columnar tree, such as a conifer, can be used to emphasize the textural appeal of the foliage.

A principal application is lighting stone or brick walls. Placing the luminaire close to the wall will light the protruding surfaces and will throw the mortar joints and imperfections in the surface into sharp relief. While grazing a wall is often achieved by uplighting, it can also be achieved by downlighting from under eaves or from wall-mounted luminaires. When using steplights to light across steps or paved areas, the functional safety requirement is complemented by highlighting the decorative appeal of the colour and texture of the building material.

Washing

Providing an even coverage of light on a wall is called 'washing' or 'wall washing' and is used for many purposes. In modern gardens with painted rendered walls lacking in texture, washing will draw attention to colour or reflect from light walls to define the space and create an intimate atmosphere. The key to this effect in a small or intimate space is to use a low level of lighting, which contributes to a subtle ambience. The luminaires used may be surface- or ground-recessed and may feature either reflector lamps – perhaps with frosted lenses to diffuse the light – or capsule lamps within separate reflectors to provide diffused light (2). Manufacturers may use terms such as 'wall washer' or 'mini-flood' for such luminaires.

Washing can also be used to light hedges or conifer screens to provide visual links or backdrops to individually lit features, such as statues or urns. On a larger scale, wall-washing from ground-mounted floodlights can be used for façades, although you should bear in mind that this technique may cause glare when you glance out of a window or walk out through a doorway. Lighting the architectural features of the building in more selective ways produces better results in residential settings. A less common method of wall-washing is to use small floodlights or diffuse downlights under the eaves of a house.

2

top: Washing light up the wall also outlines the containers and topiary. The stems and foliage of the climbers are also shadowed upwards onto the surface.

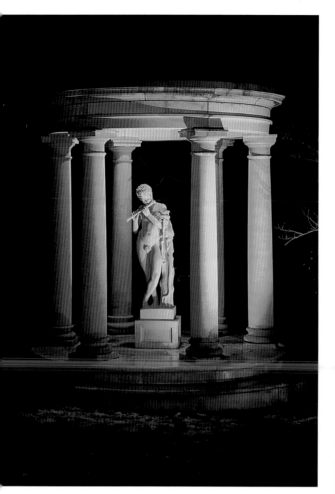

would be visually flattened by frontal lighting to the point where the feature would appear as a flat cut-out. Lighting from one side will often display this well, although this sometimes means that part of the form is lost in shadow. This can be rectified by adding another luminaire on the opposite side, either a little further away or fitted with a less bright lamp, so that infill lighting is sufficient to blank out part of the shadow without negating the textural effect of the first spotlight. Spike-mount luminaires will offer the most flexibility in balancing the lighting where two sources are used, but wall-mounted spotlights fixed to adjacent structures can be an effective alternative if you can choose from a wide enough range of lamps.

above: Uplighting the piper from within the temple is complement-ed by crosslighting from the right which emphasizes the structure.

right: Crosslighting the statue of a lady from the right suits her shy pose as well as using shadow to reveal form.

Focused down the wall of the house, such luminaires can light the façade as well as the planting, entrance and path areas below to provide security lighting.

Crosslighting

Crosslighting is another term that describes the position of the luminaire and the direction of light rather than the resulting lighting effect. It means placing the luminaire to the side of the subject so that the light travels across it **(1)**. Crosslighting a hedge by means of spotlights fitted with wide-beam lamps can result in washing or grazing effects just as effectively as uplighting from directly in front.

Crosslighting is most often used where lighting from the side will emphasize texture and form more than lighting from the front. This is particu-larly useful where the form of a light-coloured statue or relief on an urn

1

Accent lighting

Accent lighting uses directional luminaires to emphasize individual plants, focal points or other features so that they stand out within the view, either against a dark background or where a backdrop of a hedge, wall or planting is less brightly illuminated. It can be achieved by any positional technique – uplighting, downlighting or crosslighting – and from any point of origin – under water, in a tree, in the ground or on a structure. It is achieved by focusing a relatively intense beam of light on the subject but requires careful positioning and aiming to avoid the evils of over-lighting, which creates a washed-out appearance, or light spilling beyond the focal point to project ugly shadows on adjacent surfaces **(2)**.

Spotlighting

The term spotlighting is often confused with accent lighting, and quite often it is the same thing. It is usually refers to circumstances where the luminaire is placed at some distance from the subject to be lit, often because there is no nearer

practicable mounting position **(3)**. Examples could include spotlights under the eaves of a building used to illuminate focal points or paving features at ground level, or lighting the canopy of a tree from a planted border some distance from the trunk to avoid the use of a spike-mount luminaire in an intervening lawn area. Narrower, more intense 'spotlight' beams may be used to compensate for the distance from the subject or to achieve a tight circle of light around the feature (see page 20).

above: A spike-mount luminaire accent lights the wall panel to reveal relief and provide a focal point through the dark foreground planting.

below left: Spotlighting down onto an architectural plant creates a stunning focal point, an effect accentuated by leaving the surrounding planting in darkness.

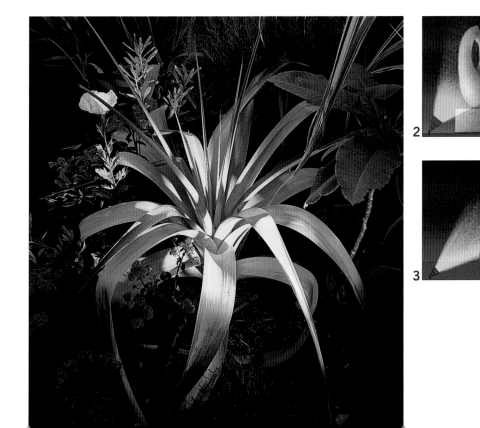

2

3

Mirroring

Mirroring is achieved quite simply by accent lighting a feature on the far side of a body of water so that its image is mirrored in the water when it is seen from a viewpoint on the patio, in the house or from a strategically placed seat **(1)**. The best subjects are those with a light colour and clear outline reflected in sharp focus on the water – for example, simple urns and classical features, such as a stone temple.

Mirroring is a simple matter of geometry. If an object is illuminated, the mirroring effect will be achieved as long as the body of water is large enough to accommodate the size of the reflection from a given viewpoint.

right: Light-coloured focal points make good subjects for mirroring in formal ponds.

below: Mirroring of these busts of Bacchus and a Bacchante in the dark water of the swimming pool is a creative alternative to leaving the pool lighting switched on.

Because it depends as much on the angle of view as it does on the size of the subject, it can even be achieved on a miniature scale on a roof garden. The mirroring will succeed only if the subject is brightly illuminated and the water is sufficiently dark. For example, a tree with a fairly dense canopy must be both uplit and receive external canopy lighting; uplighting from within the canopy is likely to be too subtle to reflect strongly in the water. The lighting must be bright enough to outweigh any moonlight or city skyglow on the surface of the water, and stray light from interior illumination or area lighting near the water must be eliminated. Underwater lighting should be avoided and lighting of adjacent areas limited in brightness. See also page 62.

1

Silhouetting

This effect occurs when a dark image of a subject is created by lighting a wall or other vertical surface behind it. While the colour and texture of the subject are hidden, the interesting shape of a small tree, an architectural plant or an object with a distinctive outline can make a fascinating focal point. An alternative is where screening plants are 'silhouetted' against a pale wall to produce a textured tableau: bamboos are particularly good subjects for this treatment. Wide diffused beams, as used in straightforward wall-washing, will give the best result. Occasionally, the effect comes not from garden lighting but from interior lighting silhouetting the exterior planting against the illuminated background of plain blinds, or perhaps *shoji* screens in a Japanese context to provide a pleasing backdrop to a terrace. Courtyards can benefit from this effect.

The halo effect

You may have read descriptions of backlighting trees to produce a silhouette effect, but this is a misinterpretation of the word silhouette (see left). If there is no illuminated background, there is no silhouette. What backlighting does is to produce a halo of light around the edges of the trunk and branches in the case of a spreading tree or the foliage outline in the case of a conifer (2). The halo shows the shape or structure of the tree and is a subtle effect against a dark background. The halo treatment is often used where there is a need to provide variety among other trees and shrubs that are lit more from the front or side. If the lighting comes from directly behind the subject, the effect may be too subtle to have any impact. It is often better to place the luminaire behind and slightly to one side of the tree to produce a more pronounced halo

below left: Uplighting the wall from behind the urn throws the phormium into silhouette against the background of textured brickwork.

2

the principal method of providing the kind of lighting we regard as essential in an outdoor room. On a patio, that might include lighting to eat or read by, to help us navigate around the table and toys, and to carry food and utensils to and from the table. Directional lighting can be used for some of these activities if there is an overhead beam to mount such luminaires on, but it can be intrusive unless done well.

We are also accustomed to area lighting around us when we are in the dining and sitting rooms, either directly from wall or ceiling luminaires or indirectly by reflection from the surrounding surfaces, and we carry this expectation with us when we go outside. It is sometimes referred to as ambient lighting, although strictly speaking ambient light in the garden at night is the sum of moonlight plus light from the sky in a city or at dusk. The point is that, in the garden setting, area lighting should be sufficiently soft, diffuse and flattering to create an ambience that is subtle, relaxing and perhaps a little romantic.

Unless ornamental techniques such as moonlighting from trees or wall

above: Low-level lighting around the balcony leaves the eye free to appreciate the vista.

below: Downlighting from between overhead beams is a subtle way of lighting an area for relaxation if the light sources are both obscured from view and limited in power.

effect on one side. It works better where light filtering up through translucent foliage, such as that of some acers, adds a more colourful effect.

Area lighting

The function of area lighting is to provide sufficient general illumination within an area so that it is possible to do whatever activity is appropriate. It is washing from under the eaves of the house are feasible, area lighting is generally achieved by the use of mains-voltage wall-mounted lights on the house or on other adjacent walls, sometimes built for that purpose. These may be supplemented by column-mounted lights or by low-level lighting from spreadlights.

Floodlighting

Floodlighting is, of course, the ultimate type of area lighting, designed to mimic the high power and bland spread of daylight **(1)**. It is often misused to light horizontally from the house, to the annoyance of neighbours and astronomers. Its main application in domestic residential premises is security lighting, where 300- to 500-watt halogen units are not uncommon. These are unnecessarily high wattages for most residential applications, particularly if they are badly focused and directed, and 150 watts is more than adequate for many domestic applications. A bit of thought about their location and focusing can make them an asset rather than a nuisance. Using small, 100- to 150-watt halogen floodlights or 50-watt

wide-beam downlights under the eaves of a two-storey house can provide adequate security lighting as well as washing the façade and lighting planting, path and entrance below. Floodlights should be focused downwards within an angle of sixty degrees from vertical to avoid light trespass and glare to neighbouring properties, paths or roads.

1

top: Downlighting from garden structures produces more subtle effects than floodlighting from house walls.

left: Interior lighting reflects from the overhead canopy to provide diffuse illumination for viewers of this cityscape.

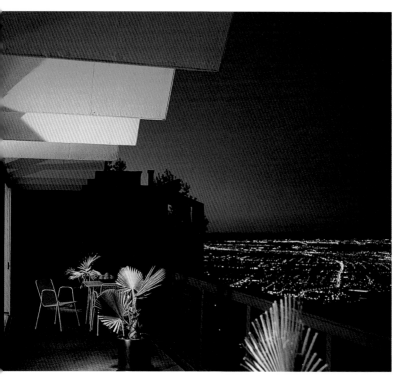

right: Recessed steplighting provides safe access without excessive visual intrusion into the surface finish.

below right: A louvred stainless steel recessed light adds a modern touch to glare-free steplighting.

Step- and vista lighting

Steplighting is a functional requirement rather than a lighting technique, but it merits separate consideration as it provides a convenient heading to discuss the discreet lighting of steps and the horizontal surfaces to or from which they lead. Where overhead lighting is not an available option, lighting at step level becomes necessary. Each individual tread should receive direct lighting, unshadowed by the riser above, from light sources shielded within the luminaire so the pedestrian is not blinded or distracted by glare while ascending the stairs (1).

Luminaires fixed in the risers of steps will be directly in the line of vision as your eyes check the route forward for your feet to follow, but this is sometimes the only available option – where there is no flanking wall, bank or balustrade, for example, or on circular staircases. It is better to provide steplighting through small lights set into, or mounted on, a flanking wall. Choose types that are characterized by shields, grilles, inset lamp housings or 'eyelid' hoods that hide the light source from passing overhead view.

Steplighting can also be useful when it is important to protect a vista – for example, when foreground lighting of steps, patio **(2)** or deck must be directed downwards so that it does not make it impossible to see a view beyond.

Spreadlighting

Manufacturers use the term spreadlight or pathlight for their products, while consumers tend to call them mushroom lights. Spreadlighting is the use of low-level luminaires to provide a glare-free, usually circular pool of light for a path, step, patio or area of low planting **(3)**. They commonly have tungsten bulbs or halogen capsule lamps of around 20 watts and provide a circle of light 2.5–4m (8–13ft) across. In many ways, spreadlighting is a last resort because the luminaires must be visible

if they are to do their job. However, where ornamental lighting techniques such as moonlighting cannot be used and where there are no walls or structures on which to mount recessed or discreet lights, spreadlights must be used to fulfil essential safety functions in lighting path and steps, as well as to fill in areas of darkness.

left: Spreadlights are a matter of taste and a last resort for path lighting. Choosing colours that blend in amongst planting makes them more acceptable.

bottom: Copper spreadlights provide pools of light around decking and low planting. Weathered copper blends well with timber and gravel.

3

1

Shadowing

The shadow of a plant or small tree can be projected onto a wall behind by placing a spotlight in front of the plant so that the light shines through the foliage towards the wall **(1)**. This simple technique uses a low-power, wide-beam lamp in a spike-mount spotlight, typically 20–35 watts. Vary the distance between the light source and the object being lit to alter the size of the image that is projected on the wall. Shadowing is an easy way of achieving maximum effect from a small tree in a newly planted courtyard garden, and may also be used to cast the shadow of water spray from a fountain.

Shadowing is usually directed at a vertical surface and its potential for paving is often overlooked. Using wall-mounted spotlights to cast the shadow of climbing or containerized plants is a way of adding dappled interest on paving in the smallest of gardens. A more novel use is to position discreet spotlights on fencing, a trellis or a

right: 'Shadowing' grasses onto the wall behind adds night-time texture to contrast with the daytime smoothness of a rendered finish.

below: Moonlighting down from the old apple tree provides dappled illumination of the spring bulbs and wild flowers below. Uplighting of the gnarled trunk connects the corona of light from the foliage to the ground below.

pergola to cast light down through architectural planting to provide shadow-enriched path or patio lighting.

Moonlighting

Trees can be excellent lighting platforms for illuminating all manner of garden features and areas below, including herbaceous and shrub borders, terraces, lawns, driveways, paths, steps and seating areas. A favourite technique is 'moonlighting' down from low-power lights fixed in a tree to shadow the lower branches and foliage onto the ground below **(2)**. This provides a wonderfully subtle, dappled lighting effect over a tree seat and is also a creative way of integrating the lawn into the lighting scene. In a small garden a halogen spotlight suspended from a branch about 5m (16ft) above the ground with a 35-watt, 60-degree lamp would be a good choice. For denser foliage or higher mounting points, move up to a 50-watt lamp, but for smaller trees reduce the power to 20 watts.

USING MOONLIGHTING	
SUBJECT TO BE LIT	**EFFECT OF MOONLIGHTING**
Planted urns	Reveals planting, while uplighting illuminates the urns below
Seating areas	Dappled light over al fresco dining area, tree seat or bench creates a romantic atmosphere
Drives	Textured lighting adds interest to adjacent planting and features
Lawns and gravelled areas	Emphasises horizontal dimensions in a natural way
Water features	Makes moving water sparkle; casts a silvery sheen onto pools; provides safety
Structures	Reveals roof shapes and tiling; provides shadow-enriched lighting through an open structure
Paths and steps	Provides natural-looking safety lighting; illuminates features along the way
Planting	Displays upward-facing flowers; provides contrast to uplighting; illuminates borders in a natural way
Statues	Illuminates upward-facing subjects that uplighting would leave in shadow

2

If the light source is positioned 6 or 7m (20–23ft) above ground, maintenance may become more difficult, so discharge light sources (metal halide or mercury vapour) are usually preferred because of their longer lamp life. Using 'cooler' discharge lamps of 4000–4500K colour temperature will also give you the slightly blue light of true moonlight, an effect you can also achieve with halogen fixtures by inserting a pale blue filter.

It is especially important to ensure that fittings are high enough above a walkway or seating area and not so bright as to invite an upward glance, which will only perceive glare. Internal honeycomb louvres can help to shield the light source from view, and glare guards are essential for fixtures directed away from the trunk. In the latter case, fittings must be directed downwards, within a maximum of 30 degrees angle from the vertical to avoid glare towards viewpoints or neighbours.

Moonlighting from a tree should be accompanied by uplighting of the trunk to anchor the tree to the ground, avoiding an impression of glowing foliage floating above the ground. This combination plays down the sources of light in the tree to a pleasing glow in the canopy where the up- and downlighting beams meet. Where the lights are located below the lowest branches, the effect is downlighting to apply a wash of light, rather than dappled light, onto the area below.

MOONLIGHTING SMALL AREAS

In small gardens, and even on balconies and roof gardens, the moonlighting effect can be imitated by placing spotlights on walls or structures above climbers or planted urns so that the foliage's shadow falls onto the ground below.

Lighting
garden features

above: Subtle uplighting preserves the serenity of this oriental garden while underwater lighting provides a charismatic central focus.

Of all the features in the garden, water is the one that most invites the use of lighting. Still, dark pools, rippling streams or cascading fountains and waterfalls present unparalleled opportunities for the creative and subtle use of light. Individual plants are also ideal subjects for lighting, whether it is the graceful form of an upright tree or the large, dramatic foliage of a shrub or perennial. Few gardens have no structures that can be lit – pergolas, summerhouses and arbours, for example, are all possible subjects. The structure and architecture of the house itself can be lit to emphasize striking features or disguise less attractive ones.

Water features

Whether moving or still, water always takes centre stage in a garden-lighting scheme. The trickling water of a stream, the rush of a waterfall, the sparkle of a fountain and the sheen of light on still water are all mesmeric in their own ways. At night, water contributes a magical range to the palette of garden-lighting effects, for, if creative garden lighting is about painting with light, then water provides the most varied of canvases.

Moving water

Some applications involve uplighting from still water but these tend to be the exception, and the main interests in lighting lie in exploiting two properties of water – refraction and reflection. Refraction is the property by which light is bent as it passes through the surface of water. It poses no real problems for lighting upwards from under still water because the luminaire can be simply adjusted to point the beam in the right direction. If the surface of the water is moving – because it is disturbed by a nearby waterfall or the cascade from a fountain, for example – the refraction at the water surface is continuously varied and the light coming up through the moving water is similarly varied, the light beam being bent at random,

producing a shimmering lighting effect. If we light a wall fountain, in particular, the whole scene becomes one of light dancing on the wall, the fountain and any adjacent planting.

Still water

The reflection of a statue, focal point or specimen tree in dark, still water can create a stunning but tranquil scene. It involves a relatively simple technique and can be applied to any swimming pool, lake or smaller pond. Lighting a strongly outlined subject or architectural feature on the far side of the pool produces an image that is reflected on the water in the foreground. This is also an very creative way of using a body of water that cannot be used for underwater lighting.

Complex water features

Water features that combine many different lighting opportunities within one area are found only in larger gardens. Within a complex design many ideas that are, individually, applicable to a wide range of features come together. Sophisticated lighting

above: Commercial landscape lighting techniques, including 'glitter' lighting of structures and colourful underwater lighting of water features, are inappropriate for most residential settings.

left: Underwater uplighting in a ring around the fountain catches the sparkling water falling from the fountain bowl. Crosslighting from outside the water feature reveals the upper features.

above: Complex lighting in and around this large pond includes underwater uplighting of waterfalls, lighting of planting which is reflected in darker areas of water and underlighting the bridge. The overall effect is perhaps a little fussy and over-bright.

design is achieved by looking at individual parts and the appropriate lighting effects and then by integrating them into a complete design.

Underwater lighting

Underwater uplighting of moving water, for example, a simple waterfall or fountain using a waterproof underwater spotlight is a common and effective technique. Glistening water and the shimmering light projected by underwater lighting through moving water can be fascinating. The light adds the dimension of movement to otherwise still surfaces around the central cascade, and, even where there is no feature operated by a submersible pump, the rippling of water by the wind can be enough to provide interesting movement.

Fountains

Where a fountain is only a gush of water propelled upward by an underwater jet, the foaming water is the feature to be lit. Positioning an underwater light immediately next to the source of the water spout will make sure that it is lit while concealing the light source within the luminescence of the foaming water. Often, however, a fountain is more than just the sparkle of falling water: the origin of the water flow may be a statue or another ornamental feature rather than just a piece of copper pipe. In that case, the design needs to adopt some of the principles of statue lighting, particularly the need to avoid strong shadows by lighting upwards from too close to the feature.

Another consideration may apply with regard to to tiered fountains. Lighting a fall of water from a basin into the base pool is only part of the job; lighting the statue or feature that fills the upper tier basin may require the lamps to be moved to the edge of the lower pool in order to maximize

left: The 'sunburst' wall fountain provides a perfect focus for lighting upward from the cobble-filled basin.

the coverage of the upper feature. In larger tiered fountains it may be necessary to use two sets of luminaires. One of them will uplight the fall of water from the upper basin or basins, the other will sit either on the outer edge of the base pool or within the upper basin to light the feature from which the water flow originates. In most fountain applications in private gardens, 35- to 50-watt lamps are the norm.

Wall fountains

The need to avoid heavy shadow also applies in lighting wall-mask fountains, so avoid placing the luminaires underneath the water spout. The ideal technique is to position the luminaire with a narrow- or medium-beam lamp so that light appears to travel up the water spout to accent the mask against the surrounding surface. Alternatively, a wider-beam lamp in a luminaire mounted further to the front of the basin or pool below may be used as a compromise to avoid ugly shadows. While wider beam lamps may be preferred for wall masks mounted on ornamental walls or to produce a wider area of shimmering light from below moving water, narrower beams will emphasize the water flow and mask.

For larger wall fountains or those that feature several spouts, the approach can be more complex. Accent lighting of individual spouts while using lower-power, wider-beam lamps to provide an overall wash can be effective. Providing the lights sit reasonably close to the surface of the water, 20-watt lamps should be powerful enough to illuminate most wall fountains.

below: Uplighting from the lower pool is complemented by lighting of the upper feature from inside the tiered basin.

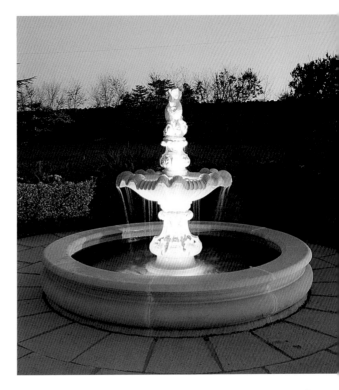

LIGHTING A WALL-FOUNTAIN

Positioning the light at the front of the pool will provide interesting shadows on the features of the lion mask while avoiding creating a bulging shadow above the mask. The light is mounted just below the water surface, so that the pump and cabling are left in darkness below, while the sparkle of the water falling is not clouded by a light beam struggling to emerge from the depths of the pond. The pipework and cables are ducted through the wall above water level and hidden under the coping. The junction box for the power supply to the pump and the transformer (suitable for outdoor use) for the underwater light are hidden behind the wall.

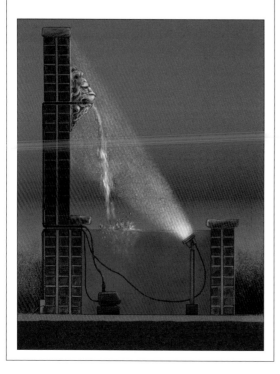

Still water

Underwater lighting is sometimes used to light upwards from the bottom of a still pool or one without a central cascade to provide an overall luminescence that emphasizes the shape of the pool. This is particularly effective in a strongly geometric design. Using frosted lenses and locating the luminaires at the bottom of the pool helps to diffuse the beams when there is no foaming spout to mask the light source. Alternatively, lighting recessed into the side walls, as in swimming pools, or set on planting shelves to crosslight the pond and illuminate marginal planting can be used. This works well only where the interior surface of the pool is smooth and dark or has a decorative or tiled finish, because the lighting will inevitably light the pool's interior.

If butyl liner is used, folds and creases will show up and mar the view. Pumps and filters may also be illuminated by badly positioned crosslighting luminaires. Once marginal planting has died back in winter, the liner is the only feature to catch the eye. To avoid this, the underwater lighting should be on a separate switch so that it can be turned off, or treat still ponds as reflecting pools and highlight planting, a rock garden or a statue on its margins so that they are mirrored in the water.

WATER CLARITY AND COLOUR

Good underwater lighting depends on the clarity of the water: water that is full of algae will reward you with a dull green or yellow glow when you switch on the lights. The success of the lighting depends, therefore, on the quality of the filtration system and on your overall management of the pond. Some slight discoloration of the water is quite common, even in a well-filtered pool, and inserting a pale blue filter in the lighting sometimes helps to correct this, giving the water a fresher look and making the marginal planting look healthy. A deeper blue filter can create an azure lagoon, but do not use this in lighting that is directed towards stone fountain features unless you do not mind if the statuary looks anaemic. Underwater lighting in natural and informal pools is rarely effective because the water is not usually clear. For such features, creating an effect with a mirrored feature or lighting marginal planting with land-based spotlights to produce reflections in the water will make better use of the both the pool and the lighting.

Positioning underwater lights

Unless the underwater lights are used for uplighting in a still pond, locating lights in the bottom of a pond can be less than effective. Murkiness can mask light output; oxygenating weed can quickly grow over the luminaires; pumps, piping and filters are often revealed; and uplighting using a narrower-beam lamp may be undermined by the effects of refraction. Locating lights separately from the pump usually provides better lighting opportunities. The best way to uplight a feature fountain or wall fountain is to position the underwater light so that the front lens is about 15cm (6in) below the water surface, where water movement helps to hide the light source.

In shallower water features it is essential that there is enough depth in which to submerge and conceal the body of the luminaire. Some models rely on water cooling to maintain lamp temperature and life, and so should be positioned at least 5cm (2in) below the surface (check the manufacturer's instructions. This can usually be achieved by locating the luminaire in a planting basket, fixed to a block on a planting shelf, or by constructing a support from plastic plumbing parts ballasted into a concrete base.

MOUNTING UNDERWATER LIGHTS

In shallow ponds (below left), fasten the underwater light's mounting bracket to a paver or block with a brass screw. Place one or two pavers or blocks underneath it, or place the block-mounted light on a marginal planting shelf, so the top of the light is 5–15cm (2–6in) below the surface (check the specifications on the packaging for the minimum depth of water). Attaching a brass chain to the block and hooking it onto the side of the pond is one way of making it easier to retrieve the block-mounted light for lamp changing without damaging the cable by pulling on it.

In larger, deeper ponds (below right), rather than standing the lamp on a tall pile of bricks, a plastic plumbing pipe ballasted in a concrete block provides an effective anchor for the lamp. It is also a good method for ensuring that the lamp is at exactly the correct depth below the surface, as the pipe can easily be trimmed to the right length. Fix the lamp to a stop-end plumbing fitting of the same diameter as the pipe; this can easily be removed to allow the luminaire to be raised above water for occasional lamp replacement, instead of lifting the heavy block of concrete up through the water.

MIRRORING

When an object is illuminated beyond an area of water, the inverted image of the object will be reflected in the dark surface when viewed from the other side of the pond or lake. Whether the reflection of the object will fit within the frame of the water's edge depends on the size of the object, the area of water in which its image can be reflected and the angle of view. The angle of view will be affected by proximity to, and elevation above, the water's edge. To see if this will work in your pond, light a 'test' feature with powerful flash lights and move it around to experiment until you get the reflection you seek from a window, conservatory or deck. This technique is used in ponds without moving water; the effect would be completely spoiled by ripples, and it also works best when there are no plants to obscure the view of the water surface.

Lighting fish ponds

Mounting lights nearer to the surface, rather than at the bottom of the pond, has another benefit if there are fish: they are attracted to the illumination at night and stay active. Lighting koi ponds requires special attention to lighting, especially where there are valuable, prized specimens; smooth, fully recessed lighting is recommended.

Mirroring

The dark surface of still water provides a surface on which a magical array of lighting effects can be reflected. 'Mirroring' is the process of lighting a subject on the far side of a pond so that it is reflected in the dark, still water. It is especially useful if the water is not clear enough for underwater lighting or if such lighting would be difficult to use without showing wrinkles in a butyl liner.

The mirroring effect is particularly effective for subjects with well-defined outlines, such as an urn, a statue or a strong architectural feature, but it can also be used with trees if the body of water is large enough. Trees must be boldly lit on the outside of the canopy for this effect to work well, and the more subtle effect of uplighting may lack sufficient impact to reflect strongly on the water. A small statue can be lit for reflection in a smaller pond, where spotlights can also be used to crosslight marginal planting, creating reflections in the water.

Mirroring can be used as a winter lighting effect in some gardens. A lily pond will be covered by leaves and flowers in summer and may be lit from the side for horticultural display. In winter, when the lilies die away, the crosslighting is switched off on a separate circuit to provide the dark mirror for the illuminated feature. Mirroring is also a refreshing alternative to underwater lighting in swimming pools. That should be on a separate circuit from the garden lighting so that it can be switched off to allow garden features to be mirrored in the water.

Bridges and stepping stones

The fascination water exerts on the human spirit draws people to move close to water. Safe lighting of pond edges and adjacent paths is a self-evident safety requirement but lighting other forms of access, especially across water, may need even more thought.

Stepping stones across a stream, pond or rill can be lit by placing luminaires that shoot narrow beams of light alongside to mark the way ahead. This not need be too bright – a narrow-beam 20-watt lamp will probably suffice – as long as the underwater light has a guard above it, or a grid across, the lens to shield the lamp glare. Simple plank bridges can be dealt with by placing underwater lights under the bridge to shine out on either side and define the edges. Avoid this technique in a pond with a wrinkled butyl liner.

Most bridges are features in themselves, as well as being a means of access, and they demand to be lit as such, and doing so is often all that is needed to light the way across. Just as lighting shrubs along a path marks the way along the route, so lighting a

above: The columns of this classical temple are uplit by 20-watt spotlights, hidden among the planting. Mellow, indirect lighting of the interior, created by bouncing light from spotlights off the ceiling, adds depth to the view.

left: The strong colour and structure of this oriental bridge produce a defined reflection in the water of this natural pond, which is not clear enough for underwater lighting. Spike-mount spotlights are positioned close to each end of the bridge, hidden in planting.

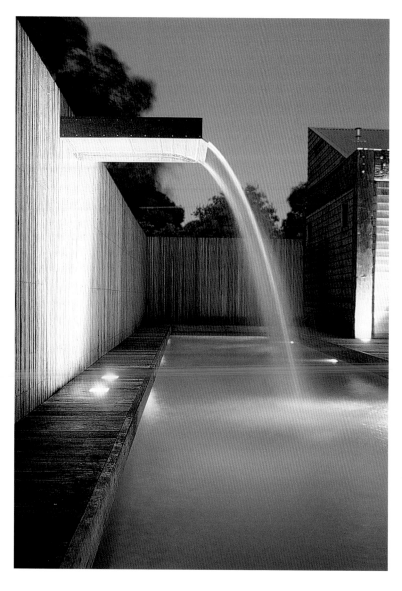

right: Uplighting the plank walls and timber structures provides an architectural framework for recessed crosslighting of this azure lagoon. The sheet of falling water receives light from the luminaires recessed into the decking, as well as from underwater lighting in front.

bridge often provides sufficient illumination to define the positions of the horizontal pathway, vertical structure and water's edge. Obvious surface-mounted lights on the bridge structure are ugly, although small copper spotlights can often be acceptable because they weather attractively to blend with timber structures. Alternatively, spiking a spotlight into the bank close to each end of a bridge can light the structure well. Setting the lights at an acute angle will usually hide the light source from view as pedestrians cross the bridge, while using glare guards and internal glare louvres will control glare on the approaches to the bridge.

If walkway lighting is required, products that can light under a handrail or from the interior uprights can be used, but these need to be carefully positioned so they do not protrude into the walkway or intrude into the daylight view of the bridge. Sometimes, spotlights mounted under the bridge shine down onto the water beneath and around it, and this can certainly be attractive where there are interesting rocks or plants to flatter the water area below. Some care may be needed to make sure that light bounced off the water surface does not become glare from another viewpoint. Although lighting emphasizes sparkle in water, sparkle and glare are two sides of the same coin, and light glancing off sheets of water can sometimes be unpredictable. Moonlighting from waterside trees is an alternative and much more natural-looking way of lighting routes around and over water.

Waterfalls

Waterfalls offer a timeless fascination in the natural landscape and lose none of their appeal when they are mimicked, even in unnatural interpretations, in our own gardens. Whether the water flows over a rocky precipice in a tumbling cascade or flows in a shimmering sheet over a metal chute or the flat edge of machined slate, the sparkle and luminescence as it falls into a basin below demand emphasis by lighting at night. The underwater spotlight is usually best located immediately below the entry point of the cascade of the water into the pool beneath so that it will be shielded among the foaming luminescence while the light beam is directed up the flow of water to create prismatic effects.

If lighting is placed in front of the waterfall, it tends to pass through the flow and light the area behind it without picking up the essential sparkle

of the water; and, if the flow is a sheet of smooth water, lighting from the front might just bounce off the water 'mirror' at an angle to cause unpredictable glare. Where there is an interesting rock formation behind the waterfall, moving the luminaire slightly behind the cascade can create the illusion of a rock grotto with a sparkling curtain in front. Underwater luminaires must be mounted on brackets, which can be tightened to maintain focus, and fixed on secure supports, which can withstand buffeting from water turbulence. The support must be moveable so that the optimum position can be achieved and so that the luminaire can be removed from the water for occasional lamp-changing and maintenance. Even in the cleanest water feature there will be a certain amount of encrustation resulting from waterborne salts and algae; this will have to be removed from time to time.

Rock gardens

Rock gardens are frequently found alongside waterfalls, and they can form the backdrop to the focal point of the waterfall. By their nature, rock gardens recede from the water's edge,

above: Underwater uplighting of the waterfalls is complemented by 'in-fill' lighting of the rocks and planting which can't be reached by underwater luminaires.

with a sheer area of rock constructed for the main event – the water dropping down the face. The receding levels of the rocks mean that any underwater light placed to uplight the waterfall from below will merely cast the upper rocks – and any planting at the upper levels – into complete shadow. The solution is to place extra spotlights around the lower pool and sides of the rock feature so that they will either provide lower-level infill lighting of areas cast into shadow by the underwater lighting, or light planting and additional ornaments, as secondary focal points.

Whichever blend of secondary or supplementary lighting is appropriate, the direction and intensity of the lighting should not compete with the waterfall as the primary focal point nor should it blank out the light that shimmers on the rock face. This may seem expensive, but the low-budget approach of placing a powerful, wide-beam lamp at the front of the pool to light the waterfall and rockery in one fell swoop will simply result in a boring, flat scene relieved only by a bit of sparkle.

Streams

Streams can make beautiful illuminated features. A meandering stream will enhance a moonlight walk and contrast with a raised deck or other linear feature. Planning the lighting in advance of construction can be difficult because the final look of the feature will owe much to the positioning of the rocks, falls and planting, and to the skill of the landscape contractor in creating a natural-looking landscape. Planning for a network of cable ducts under the stream will make it easier to finalize the lighting design once the rocks, pools and falls are seen in reality rather than on a plan.

Stream features can lack the depth of water in which to hide underwater lighting, so remote lighting techniques are often used. Moonlighting from trees

CAMOUFLAGING LUMINAIRES AROUND WATER FEATURES

It is far less easy to light a stream when there are no trees to act as lighting platforms for the moonlighting effect. Nothing spoils the naturalistic effect of a stream feature more than visible light fixtures, so close attention to camouflaging the positions of luminaires and the fixtures themselves is paramount. Using steplights mounted on low flanking walls or tucked under the edge of decking may be one way of hiding the light sources. If ground-mounted lights are used, small, green, spike-mount spotlights (with glare guards if they are near a pathway) may be hidden among streamside planting to light an area of rock, a

pool, a cluster of marginal planting or a small waterfall where there is insufficient depth for an underwater light. These provide points of emphasis, either used alone or to blend with moonlight if the feature consists of a succession of focal points. A series of 20-watt wide-beam halogen spotlamps, perhaps with frosted lenses to diffuse the beams in close-up lighting situations, works best.

Where spike-mounting is not possible because there is a butyl liner, wedging waterproof lights among flanking rocks is another alternative, possibly using cast brass or bronze luminaires, which will weather to blend in with rocky surrounds. If there is no diffused lighting from trees, other means of infill lighting will be needed to link any spotlit areas. This might involve low-power, probably 20-watt, halogen 'mini-floodlights' mounted on stakes hidden in adjacent planting areas. As a last resort, it might involve using spreadlights to provide circular pools of light, although stem-mounted pathlights with a 180-degree distribution would be better, provided you can camouflage the luminaires. These cast light gently across an area, while leaving the area behind in darkness.

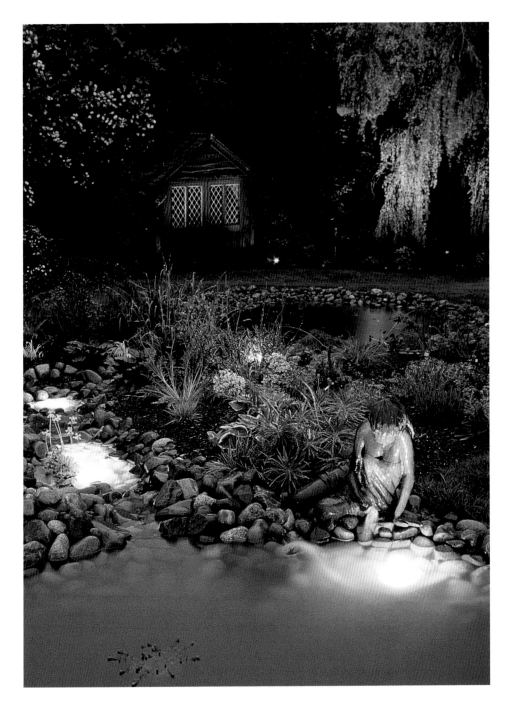

is a good option because it is a natural-looking effect and removes the difficulty of hiding ground-mounted luminaires and ensuring that they produce no directional glare. The effect produced by moonlighting is both wide-spreading and diffused, so the lighting is not patchy and represents good value for a gardener working to a limited budget. Most importantly, it produces a silvery sheen on the surface of stiller water.

Small water features

The bubbling of water can add a certain something to even the smallest garden, whether it is a courtyard, balcony or roof garden. At night lighting brings an intimacy to such areas that is much more difficult to achieve in many larger settings, and in this sort of setting glittering water acts as a magnet to the eye. Small features should be subtly lit to suit their size.

above: Lighting a meandering stream will add interest to an evening walk.

Upright water features

If it is upright, uplight it. Following this simple rule is usually the best approach because the vertical dimension should be emphasized to enhance the effect of the moving water. Small water features of this kind, such as cobble fountains, are often prefabricated and have a small base reservoir. Water drops onto a cobble, flint or pebble layer that masks a supporting grid over the reservoir. This cosmetic layer over the grid is ideal for hiding a waterproof uplight: perhaps a black one among slate or a brass one that will age to blend in among cobbles. In most situations 20-watt lamps will be sufficient, and you may need to use an internal glare louvre if the feature is close to a patio or window.

To uplight urn water features, where the water trickles down the side of the urn to be re-circulated and pumped back up inside, an underwater light inside the urn is sometimes used to provide shimmering uplighting on an overhead canopy. However, uplighting

above: Underwater uplighting of the waterfall produces shimmering illumination of the brick structure, while crosslighting of the water staircase adds a sparkling sheen to the trickling of the water running down.

right: Illumination of the wall feature leaves unlit planting to frame the view with silhouettes.

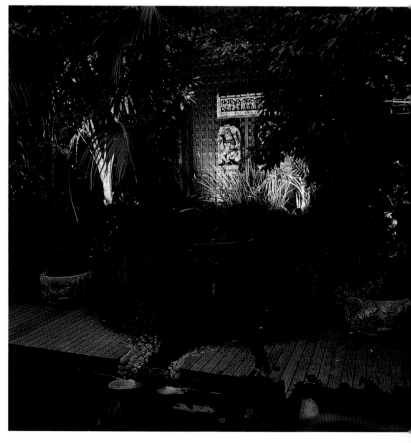

the trickling water on the outside is more effective. Do not place the light too close to the side of the urn or you will get a 'dinner plate' of light as the beam does not have the opportunity to spread. Position the light a little way back, use the widest beam lamp available and fit a frosted lens to diffuse the beam. A 'spread' lens is a useful device that will turn a circular beam into an elongated oval or rectangle to help with lighting taller or wider objects from close range.

Low water features

Small, low water features are best lit from above or the side. If there is an overhead or adjacent structure, focus a surface-mounted spotlight with a 20- to 35-watt lamp in a narrow to medium beam spread on it. This will provide accent lighting that will make the feature stand out from its surroundings, while leaving adjacent surfaces, such as fences, which you do not necessarily want to light, in the dark. A 50-watt, narrow or very narrow beam may be needed to spotlight the feature from a more distant mounting point, such as under the eaves of the house.

If no overhead lighting position exists, spreadlighting may be the next best choice. However, if possible, use a 180-degree pathlighting product to diffuse light towards the feature while disguising the source of the light. The use of pole-mounted spotlights works only if the luminaires can be disguised.

Water features, such as millstones, urns or bubble fountains, can be downlit from a wall or pergola, or illuminated by a spreadlight or area lighting source tucked into adjacent planting. For example, using a copper light with a very small head and a shield to restrict the lighting to a 180-degree arc allows a low-level subject to be lit without light being projected towards a viewpoint. Where you need a ground-level light source that diffuses light rather than projecting a beam, especially if the available lighting position is close to the subject, a spike-mount spreadlight, steplight or a miniature low-voltage floodlight mounted on a short stake are options to consider.

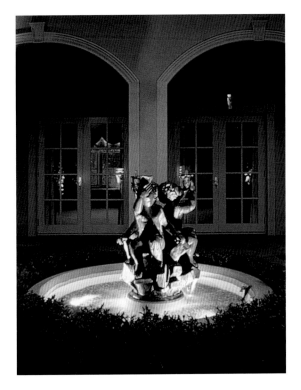

above: Underwater uplighting of the fountain from several directions makes this striking feature a fitting focal point in the centre of the courtyard.

SAFETY AROUND WATER

Like electricity, water is a potential hazard in the garden, but only if it is not properly integrated into the garden design and properly managed. The electricity supply used for pumps and filters as well as for lighting must have proper circuit protection. Water itself can be dangerous in the garden, and not just to children; lighting has an important role to play in promoting the safe use of water features at night. Lighting the body of water from beneath, to show where firm ground ends, is one option. In addition, lighting paths, bridges, stepping stones and banks so that the water's edge and safe routes around or across the feature are clearly visible is an essential safety requirement.

Trees

A tree provides a unique opportunity to add vertical emphasis and drama to the evening landscape, and illuminated trees can produce stunning results, adding scale to the nightscape whether they are primary features, seen directly or mirrored in the dark water of a pond or lake, or secondary features, acting as backdrops to a statue or formal feature.

Lighting techniques

Uplighting is the most common technique used for lighting trees, but the position and type of light fixture and choice of lamp type and power can produce varying results. You need to assess the tree's size, canopy density, structure, shape, colour, textures and position, and there are more choices possible for the type of lamp and lighting than for almost any other subject in the garden.

Deciding which trees to light and which techniques to use requires careful consideration. Lighting large trees close to an exterior viewpoint, such as the patio, may have a majestic impact if the luminaire can be shielded from view. However, the same tree close to the house may be difficult to see easily from a window. Conversely, small trees some distance from the house may be seen only as a blob of light from a window. The farther a tree is from the viewpoint the more brightly it must be lit if it is not to fade into the distance, while closer subjects catch your eye instead.

far right: The translucent leaves of *Acer Palmatum* 'Bloodgood' will glow a brilliant red as light filters upwards from a 50 watt uplight situated below.

right: Laburnum flowers bloom for a short time and make a stunning spectacle under lighting, but you may wish to focus the spotlight on more interesting companion planting for the rest of the year.

Choosing subjects to light

Just because a particular tree is a favourite, it does not necessarily mean that it is a good candidate for lighting, because any structural faults will be glaringly obvious. Light the side that is not wind-damaged, for example, or light it less brightly than other subjects in the garden so that it becomes a secondary focal point.

An alternative is to use it as a lighting platform to moonlight down onto the ground, transfering attention to a lawn, patio or feature below

(see pages 52–3). Remember that it is still important to uplight the trunk of a tree to some extent to tie it to the ground or the moonlighting may make the canopy appear to hover in mid-air.

In some gardens there may be many specimens vying for attention. Do not be tempted to light them all, or to light many of them in the same way. Pick out a few really good specimens and go for contrast and light them from the front or different sides, or use different lighting intensities or lamp colour temperatures to reinforce the different foliage. Equally, do not try for variety where none should exist; an avenue of

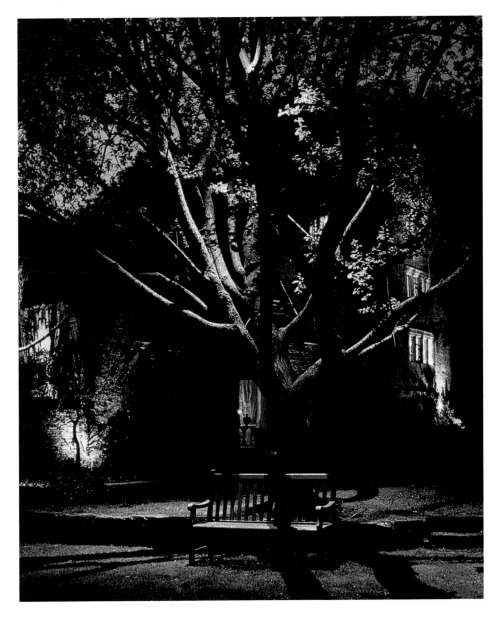

trees can only be lit as an avenue of trees – uniformly – unless you are attempting the dangerous game of trying to create false perspectives.

Tree colour

The colour of a tree will be an important consideration when you are selecting lighting, but it is even more important for smaller, ornamental trees in smaller gardens, where the overwhelming grandeur of a larger tree is not the prime factor. Some good specimen trees are listed on pages 70–71 together with the characteristics that make them appropriate for lighting.

There are a few general guidelines to bear in mind.

Light-coloured foliage, bark, flowers or berries will always stand out with relatively low-powered lighting. The same is true for trees with colourful, translucent leaves, especially if they are red or orange, such as some acers and liquidambar in autumn. Avoid over-lighting these subjects, or the effect may be overpowering; choose fixtures that you can trade down to a lower-wattage lamp if necessary. Darker foliage and bark may need at least two to three times as much lighting as light-coloured subjects for the same sort of

above: Moonlighting down through the open structure of a deciduous tree throws a strong shadow of the branch structure onto the ground below. Uplighting of the trunk could link the two areas together more positively.

TREES FOR LIGHTING

TREE	CHARACTERISTICS AS A GOOD LIGHTING SUBJECT
Acer capillipes Snake-bark maple	Striped bark and bright green leaves, which turn brilliant orange and red in autumn
Acer japonicum 'Aconitifolium' Japanese maple	Elegant habit and deeply dissected leaves, which turn ruby-red or crimson in autumn
Acer negundo 'Variegatum' Variegated box maple	Fast-growing, small to medium-sized tree with green leaves with white edges
Acer palmatum 'Bloodgood' Japanese maple	Deep reddish-purple translucent leaves make a fiery spectacle when uplit
Acer platanoides 'Drummondii' Variegated Norway maple	Striking, large tree with large green leaves with a broad, creamy white margin
Acer saccharinum Silver maple	Deeply divided, light green leaves with silver undersides turn butter yellow in autumn
Alnus glutinosa 'Imperialis' Alder	Lovely cultivar with deeply divided leaves
Arbutus unedo Strawberry tree	Small tree with dark evergreen leaves, white flowers and red 'strawberry' fruit
Betula pendula 'Laciniata' Cutleaf silver birch	Tall, slender tree with a silvery bark, pendulous branches and deeply cut leaves
Betula pendula 'Youngii' Young's weeping birch	Graceful, umbrella-shaped, weeping tree with attractive foliage and white bark
Carpinus betulus 'Fastigiata' Upright hornbeam	Medium-sized tree; the columnar shape broadens to almost round as it matures
Castanea sativa 'Albomarginata' Variegated sweet chestnut	Fast-growing, large tree with long, toothed, shiny green leaves with white margins
Catalpa bignonioides Indian bean tree	Umbrella-shaped tree with large, heart-shaped leaves and white and purple flowers
Cedrus libani subsp. *libani* Cedar of Lebanon	Open structure with horizontal branches and tufts of dark green needles
Cercidiphyllum japonicum Katsura	Medium-sized tree, usually grown for its autumn colour
Cornus controversa 'Variegata' Wedding cake tree	Beautiful small tree with horizontal branches of pendulous green and white leaves
Cryptomeria japonica Elegans Group Japanese cedar	Elegant conifer with brownish-green curving 'leaves', which turn coppery bronze in autumn
Cupressus sempervirens Stricta Group Italian cypress	Tall, slim, dark green columns, most effective when grouped to form living sculptures
Fagus sylvatica 'Dawyck' Dawyck's beech	Columnar form of the European beech; the bronze-leaved form is *F. s.* 'Dawyck's Purple'

SPECIMEN TREES

TREE	CHARACTERISTICS AS A GOOD LIGHTING SUBJECT
Fagus sylvatica 'Pendula' Weeping beech	Dramatic weeping tree with autumn colour
Fraxinus excelsior 'Pendula' Weeping ash	In winter the downwash of weeping branches turns the tree into a living sculpture
Gleditsia triacanthos 'Sunburst' Honey locust	Fern-like, glossy golden-yellow foliage in spring
Ilex aquifolium 'Argentea Marginata' Silver-margined holly	Shiny variegated leaves reflect light brilliantly
Laburnum alpinum 'Pendulum' Weeping laburnum	Weeping branches are spectacular with hanging racemes of yellow flowers
Ligustrum lucidum 'Tricolor' Variegated Chinese privet	Evergreen tree with glossy green leaves with creamy white edges and creamy white flowers
Liquidambar styraciflua Sweet gum	Conical tree with glossy leaves that turn purple, orange and red in autumn
Liriodendron tulipifera 'Fastigiatum' Upright tulip tree	Columnar when young, turning more ovoid with age; large green leaves turning gold in autumn
Paulownia tomentosa Foxglove tree	Open branches carry clusters of heliotrope-blue foxglove-like flowers in spring
Populus x *candicans* 'Aurora' Balsam poplar	Large, balsam-scented green leaves boldly variegated with pink-tinged, cream blotches
Prunus serrula Cherry	Polished mahogany-coloured bark
Prunus x *yedoensis* 'Shidare-yoshino' Yoshino weeping cherry	Graceful spreading tree with hanging branches covered with blossom in early spring
Pyrus salicifolia 'Pendula' Weeping willow-leafed pear	Weeping branches of silvery foliage
Robinia pseudoacacia 'Umbraculifera' Mophead false acacia	Naturally rounded shape and soft, light green foliage
Salix babylonica var. *pekinensis* 'Tortuosa' Contorted willow	Small tree with twisting stems and pendulous leaves that turn yellow in autumn
Salix caprea 'Kilmarnock' Kilmarnock willow	Weeping tree with silky male catkins
Sorbus vilmorinii	Arching branches with clusters of blue-green, fern-like leaves turning red-purple in autumn
Taxus baccata 'Fastigiata' Irish yew	Strong, upright shape; the golden form is *T. b.* 'Aurea'

effect, and if you want to light a copper beech or purple sycamore be prepared to use five times (or more) as much lighting power. Even then, you will not see much of the very dark foliage. Instead try to exploit its darkness by lighting up through the centre of the tree so that the dark foliage is silhouetted against the inner glow. Rather than trying for the same lighting effect on very different subjects, light them to emphasize their differences and make a feature of the contrast.

If the tree's glory is short-lived, make sure that the tree is at least acceptable in the lighting scene for the rest of the year. Apple blossom and the yellow flowers of laburnum may be stunning for a while, but will such trees still look good under lighting for the rest of the year? In some cases, refocusing the spotlight on companion planting provides an opportunity to ring the changes. In other cases, explore

alternative concepts as well: can the orchard become a moonlit walk, for example? Always keep the direction and distance of the viewpoint in mind; uplighting trees for interesting bark colour or texture is worthwhile only if they are close enough to a viewpoint for it to be appreciated. If they are not, work with the shape and canopy to grab the attention instead.

Tree shape
The power of the light source and whether it is focused into a narrow or wide beam will determine how far up the tree the light can travel (see page 76). The key question is whether the structure of the tree and the density of the canopy will prevent the light from reaching this far. Stand back and assess the tree's shape and geometry and whether it limits the possible positions of one or more uplights: are there large roots, surrounding paving, nearby water or

UPLIGHTING TREES
SHAPE AND STRUCTURE

The method of lighting trees depends principally on shape and structure, as shown below by: a tree with an open structure, a tree with a dense canopy, a textured tree with a dense canopy and a mature tree with an open structure.

1 Trees with an open structure and canopy can be uplit, using spike-mount uplights hidden among planting or recessed lights in a lawn. Emphasis is on structure.

2 Trees with a dense canopy and attractive shape must be lit from outside the canopy. Use a spike-mount wide-beam spotlight or floodlight located in an adjacent border. Emphasis is on shape.

3 Trees with a dense textured canopy can be 'grazed' by uplighting near the outside of the canopy. Use a spike-mount spotlight or adjustable recessed uplight with a narrow to medium beam. Emphasis is on texture.

4 Large mature trees with open structure and denser outer foliage require a combination of uplighting the trunk with a narrow beam and the canopy with one or more under beams. Emphasis is on structure.

simply directions from which the tree must, or must not, be viewed? Remember that halogen lamp beams or the beam angles of reflectors used in discharge fittings tend to span a range of about 10 to 60 degrees, so how will beam angles 'fit' the tree? A narrow beam will obviously suit a columnar silver birch or eucalyptus, a wellingtonia or a sequoiadendron, while a large willow, with its spreading canopy, may well need more than one wide-beam unit.

Tree structure

The next consideration is structure. Will the structure of the tree allow the light to penetrate upwards? An open structure allows light to reach up through the canopy to highlight the trunk and branches. As a rule, if you can stand at the base of the trunk and look up through the canopy to the upper branches, uplighting from the base of the tree will be a successful technique.

Some trees, especially many conifers, will fail this simple test because the canopy is dense and starts at or near ground level, so uplighting from below will tend to produce a green glow that fades out long before the light has penetrated the upper reaches. For such trees, the usual treatment is 'washing' the exterior of the tree with light, although you may also be able to shoot a narrow beam up close to the trunk to add a little drama.

At the same time as assessing the openness of the tree structure to determine the feasibility of lighting it, think about the desirability of doing so. Winter, of course, will reveal the structure of a deciduous tree starkly and dramatically under lighting. The beauty of a tree with an inherently pleasing branching structure can be most effectively displayed during dormancy, but a tree with tangled or wind-damaged branches will be revealed for the eyesore that it is. In autumn and winter find other subjects in the garden to light, or light the tree selectively.

Lighting within the canopy

Uplighting will produce markedly different effects according to the position of the luminaire or luminaires in relation to the tree and the choice of lamps. Depending on the shape and size of the tree, decide if certain features need emphasis and consider how lighting inside or outside the canopy can best achieve this. When we uplight a tree from underneath we are lighting it from inside the canopy. If only one luminaire is being used, for smaller trees especially, it should be placed sufficiently close to the base of the tree to light the trunk from near the ground, but not halfway up, otherwise the tree will look as though it is floating eerily in mid-air. The lamp chosen should have a sufficiently wide beam to light a good portion of the canopy. Placing the light close to the trunk will emphasize the texture and colour of the bark, while uplighting from below will emphasize the graceful structure of an open branching tree. Lighting the structure and canopy from within also reveals them against the silhouette of the unlit outer canopy, which provides fascinating depth.

above: Uplighting in the dense foliage of a chestnut tree fades progressively through the canopy. It becomes more visible as the night sky behind it darkens.

shoot a beam of light up the trunk. Although many columnar and pyramidal trees can be lit only from outside the canopy, the position of the luminaire will determine whether shape or texture is emphasized. Placing the luminaire so that it lights up the outside of the tree from within an aiming angle of 15 degrees from the vertical will produce a grazing effect and will emphasize texture. This is within the range of internal adjustment available in many recessed uplights. Siting the luminaire further away, with an aiming angle of up to 40 degrees from the vertical, will provide a more uniform wash of light that will show more of the shape of the tree. This degree of adjustment will require spike-mounted spotlights in adjacent planting areas or adjustable surface-mount luminaires fixed to low walls or structures. Paving, roots, lawn, tree seats and swings below the tree may get in the way of your ideal choice of position and type of luminaire, so some compromises may be required.

above: The weeping branches of the willow tree sway across the uplighting beam while moonlighting illuminates the euonymus below.

below: The feathery foliage of tree ferns produces one of the most delicate and graceful lighting scenes in the garden.

Lighting outside the canopy

For larger trees a combination of two or more luminaires will be required: a narrower beam to light the trunk from near the base, and one or more wider beam units further out to light the canopy. Whether the canopy lighting uplights are placed inside or outside the canopy may depend on several factors, but principally the density of the canopy. In the case of open structure and canopy, lighting from underneath preserves the depth of internal illumination. For trees with a dense canopy positioning luminaires to light from outside is the only option. If possible retain a central narrow beam unit to

Smaller trees

For many trees up to about 10m (33ft) high, low-voltage halogen uplights of 50–100 watts, used singly or in twos or threes, will produce a stunning effect at reasonable cost. To uplight small trees use one or more spike-mounted spotlights or recessed uplights with a minimum lamp wattage of 50 watts and a beam angle to suit the tree. An angle of 24 degrees would suit a slender silver birch; 60 degrees would be appropriate for a weeping tree or spreading canopy; and 36–40 degrees would suit most tree shapes that fall in between.

Smaller specimens in walled gardens and courtyards may also be lit. Lighting a wall or hedge to silhouette a small tree in front is an interesting effect if the tree has an open structure. Alternatively, a spotlight in front can project the shadow of a tree onto the wall behind. This is a good way of using, for example, a small acer to create a big effect in a newly planted garden. It may be possible to vary the effect from season to season. You could uplight an acer during the summer that is shadowed or silhouetted in winter (see pages 47 and 52) by moving the low-voltage spotlight forwards relative to the subject or behind it to graze a wall against which the tree will be seen in dark outline. To uplight the trunk locate the fitting about 50cm (20in) from the trunk for a 50-watt wide-beam lamp and up to 1m (3ft) for a 100-watt unit.

Larger trees

For darker, denser or larger specimens, higher-power low-voltage uplights are available in both recessed and surface-mount types and use 75-watt dichroic or 75- or 100-watt metal-reflector halogen lamps. The largest trees may require more than the focused power of several 75- or 100-watt halogen reflector lamps, so light sources other than tungsten halogen may have to be considered. This is because the higher power linear halogen lamp used in floodlights is fine for applications in security lighting but is not well suited to lighting up into a tree without blasting wasted light into the night sky. So the choice lies between higher-power tungsten spotlights and discharge lamps designed for focused lighting applications.

Tungsten sources such as 300-watt PAR56 projector lamps have been widely used in the past, and their slightly yellow light can provide a warm feel to rich brown bark. On the other hand, tungsten lighting tends to give foliage a brownish tinge. It is also relatively energy inefficient and produces considerable heat, which means that it may need to be shielded to protect people from accidental contact, or require guards, which can restrict light output or accumulate litter. Of the discharge light sources, sodium lighting addresses the energy efficiency issue, but its yellow light and poor colour rendering make it a poor choice for lighting trees.

On the other hand, single-ended metal halide lamps are ideal for focused

far left: Uplighting the trunk emphasizes bark texture often missed in daylight. The proximity of paths, a pool area and nearby houses preclude lighting of the canopy from the outside, leaving an inner glow against the night sky as the legacy of lighting from below.

above left: The reflective white bark and silver underside of the foliage of a silver birch make them beautiful lighting subjects with only low power lamps.

lighting applications, are energy efficient and cooler running, and are available in different 'colour temperatures' so the colour can be matched to the needs of the subject. The lowest colour temperature, 3000K (see page 16), provides the same, slightly golden-white light as halogen lamps and tends to flatter the mid-green foliage of broadleaf trees, the lighter foliage of robinias and acacias, the silvery undersides of some foliage and the white and coloured bark of many ornamental species. However, using this warm

UPLIGHTING TREES: LAMP POWER AND BEAM ANGLE

The illustrations below show the approximate height of tree (in metres) that can be lit by the principal combinations of lamp wattage and beam angle.

above: Metal halide lamps with a 4000K blue tinged colour temperature emphasize the foliage colour of this Cedar of Lebanon.

metal halide

10° 35 watts 20m	30° 35 watts 12m	50° 35 watts 10m
10° 70 watts 25m	30° 70 watts 16m	50° 70 watts 12m
10° 150 watts 30m	30° 150 watts 25m	50° 150 watts 15m

tungsten halogen

12° 75 watts 15m	24° 75 watts 10m	36° 75 watts 7m	60° 75 watts 5m
	24° 100 watts 15m	36° 100 watts 8m	

colour to uplight trees with a blue or grey tinge to the foliage, such as some pines and cedars, tends to make them look rather grey and dusty. A simple change to a lamp with a slightly bluer, cooler colour rendering of, say, 4200K, will bring such a tree to life.

Conversely, if you have used a cooler lamp – that is one with a higher colour temperature – to uplight an oak or beech tree, the bluish tinge to the light will give the tree a ghostly feel, which can be simply corrected by changing to a warmer lamp. Metal halide luminaires rely on internal reflectors for beam control, but the fact that a metal halide lamp is physically larger than a halogen capsule means that the optical control is less refined. This has the advantage of producing a controlled central beam that can be used for lighting the trunk and branch structure and a peripheral spread to light the canopy. The uplight can, therefore, be placed farther from the trunk, making it easier to avoid the tree's roots.

Lighting large trees requires powerful luminaires that are normally associated with commercial projects, but the powerful lighting must be contained within the garden boundaries so that light does not trespass into neighbouring windows. It may also be important to light the trees from one side only – you might, for instance, want to see the tree from the house but not have it appear too boldly to the outside world. Environmentally conscious home-owners will also wish to avoid the wasteful projection of light into the sky.

Plants

Tastes in garden lighting vary widely, and nowhere is this more so than in the

---

LIGHTING TOPIARY

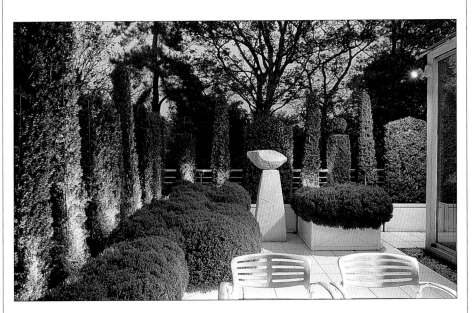

Lighting architectural planting for its inherent features is one thing, but lighting topiary is a completely different subject. It is more akin to lighting statues and focal points, and indeed that is often its role, especially in formal layouts or small gardens. Grazing up trimmed cones of box or bay can work well to emphasize texture. A second luminaire can be used to establish the shape against the darkness. Other subjects need either more space to allow for crosslighting of complex manicured shapes, or additional lighting angles to show shape fully. Mophead trees tend to look like green wine glasses if they are only uplit from underneath because there is a shadow on the top half of the sphere. To see the full shape you would need to add either downlighting from a structure or crosslighting at the height of the standards.

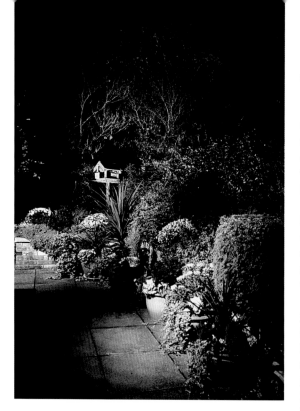

some impression of shape and space. Lighting odd objects dotted across the landscape neither gives them a sense of place nor brings any sense of unity or size to the garden. People are more comfortable when they are able to see the extent of their surroundings and lighting the planting can achieve this. Even so, being selective will pay off, light good specimens and aim for contrast. Where the border offers rich contrast and a wealth of contrasting specimen planting, then night lighting will paint a colourful tapestry.

Leaf and flower colour

Colour is an important factor in the lighting of shrub borders. Darker-leaved specimens are less reflective than lighter-coloured or variegated foliage. Lighting camellias and rhododendrons in flower can be stunning, but for the rest of the year their dark, opaque leaves are fairly boring subjects for illumination unless companion planting offers seasonal alternatives. Pale lime-green or silvery foliage stands out well under relatively low levels of lighting, while variegation adds contrast to individual plants to capture attention. Individual specimens, such as those listed on pages 80–81, may impart particularly colourful leaves, stems, flowers or berries. Flowers in pale colours, such as pink, yellow and particularly white, stand out readily under relatively low levels of light

treatment of planting. Some people prefer to light only subjects that can be classified as focal points and will include planting only if it is distinctly architectural in character. For other people, garden lighting is all about an illuminated horticultural panorama, in which focal points other than plants are irrelevant.

Fill-in lighting in shrub borders is often used to link illuminated focal points so that the eye can pan comfortably across the complete scene without having to adapt repeatedly to light and dark. It is also important to light enough of the whole garden to give

right: Moonlighting from trees onto a herbaceous border is a method of illumination used primarily for flower colour, it provides lighting coverage where dense seasonal growth would quickly mask ground-mounted luminaires.

– for example, white roses climbing over an arch can be eyecatching with a little uplighting.

Plant texture and shape

Texture is another often forgotten characteristic. It may be the texture of the plant's own leaves and stems that is highlighted by lighting, but more often it will be the overall impression of a group of plants. A screen of bamboo, for example, makes an interesting textural wall if it is grazed diagonally across the surface to bring out the pattern of its foliage, rather than uplighting to emphasize its stature. Plants with strong leaf shape offer opportunities for projecting shadows up through the plant or onto adjacent surfaces, and architectural plants can make striking features.

Uplighting and crosslighting

Uplighting tends to be the main technique used because overhead lighting positions are rare in most gardens. Spike-mounted spotlights are generally preferable, as they are less likely to be covered by lower level or groundcover planting at the front of the border than recessed uplights. There are exceptions, however. Recessed uplights are better for uplighting specimen plants in open gravel areas, for example, they may also be more resistant to damage by pets. Spike-mounted spotlights are more flexible in crosslighting shrub borders than frontal uplighting, because angling the luminaire to provide an oval beam spread along the border can increase the area of coverage, as well as increasing the contrast between light and shadow.

In winter variegated evergreens, colourful stems, berries, dried stems, foliage and seedheads provide a strong impact under lighting. In summer, lighting in borders often appears less bright than in winter, as the light is absorbed by darker, denser foliage. This is when the flexibility of low-voltage systems comes into play: lamps can be repositioned and refocused according to which specimens are of current interest. Spike-mounted uplights can be more easily manoeuvered in this context.

Downlighting and moonlighting

Where planting is dense, downlighting from trees and taller structures can introduce wide coverage and provide a contrast for uplighting. This is particularly important if flowers rather than foliage are the key to the garden design. Flowers tend to face upwards and are not seen at their best when they are lit from below, and uplighting is often masked by lower foliage. Downlighting from a pergola beam, post or wall is an effective way of highlighting the flowers of climbing plants as well as of providing overlapping lighting on to a path or patio beneath. Moonlighting down from a tree is a subtle way of lighting grass areas planted with bulbs or to light herbaceous borders where planting density conspires against uplighting of individual plants.

above left: The white panicles of pampas grass catch the light, while the slender outward-curving leaves add structure to the view.

WHITE LIGHT

The white light typical of tungsten halogen lamps and some discharge light sources flatter the natural colours of flowers and foliage to achieve a more natural-looking colour. Using a green spotlight to light a specimen plant is more likely to make it look like an artificial Christmas tree. The best choice for uplighting darker, larger shrubs in a mature garden is often a 50-watt, 36–60-degree lamp. In smaller gardens, with less mature planting or with particularly light-coloured subjects, 35-watt lamps with 36–60-degree beams will provide adequate effect. In roof gardens and small courtyards, use 20 watts to avoid over-lighting in a small space; this also reduces the risk of glare from over-bright lamps.

SPECIMEN PLANTS

PLANT	CHARACTERISTICS AS A GOOD LIGHTING SUBJECT
Acanthus mollis Bear's breeches	Large, shiny leaves and extraordinary spikes of white flowers
Acer palmatum var. *dissectum* Japanese maple	Arching branches of deeply dissected leaves provide texture and autumn colour
Aralia elata 'Variegata' Japanese angelica tree	Spreading branches of large, elegant leaves with creamy white borders
Buddleja davidii 'Harlequin' Butterfly bush	Arching branches of variegated grey-green and white leaves and deep purple flowers
Buxus sempervirens Box	Ideal plant for clipping into a topiary shapes to be lit as statuary
Cimicifuga simplex 'Brunette' Bugbane	Dark, brownish-purple shiny leaves and tall stems of white flowers in autumn
Cordyline australis 'Sundance' Cabbage palm	Large, arching, lance-shaped leaves
Cornus alba 'Elegantissimma' Red-barked dogwood	Upright scarlet red stems
Cortaderia selloana 'Sunningdale Silver' Pampas grass	Tall mound of arching leaves and upright plumes of silvery flowers
Corylus avellana 'Contorta' Corkscrew hazel	Corkscrew-like branches and yellow catkins
Cotinus coggygria 'Royal Purple' Purple smoke bush	Almost translucent, reddish-purple leaves, which turn scarlet in autumn
Cynara cardunculus Cardoon	Large, dissected, silvery-grey leaves and thick stems of large, purple, thistle-like flowers
Dicksonia antarctica Soft tree fern	Wonderful subject for lighting; hairy trunk and large, arching, fern-like leaves
Digitalis purpurea f. *albiflora* White foxglove	Tall stems of pendulous white bells arise from basal rosettes of large furry leaves
Dryopteris filix-mas Male fern	Large, arching fronds
Eryngium pandanifolium Sea holly	Silvery-green, sword-like leaves
Exochorda x *macrantha* 'The Bride'	Arching branches adorned with hanging bunches of white flowers in late spring
Fatsia japonica 'Variegata' Japanese fatsia	Architectural evergreen shrub with large, glossy green and white leaves
Gunnera manicata Giant rhubarb	Prickly stalks holding aloft almost the largest leaves of any temperate plant

SPECIMEN PLANTS

PLANT	CHARACTERISTICS AS A GOOD LIGHTING SUBJECT
Hosta sieboldiana var. *elegans* Plantain lily	Large, ribbed, blue-green leaves with pale lilac-grey flowers
Matteuccia struthiopteris Shuttlecock fern	Lime green, translucent upright fronds
Melianthus major Honey bush	Large, evergreen, serrated blue-green leaves
Miscanthus sinensis Eulalia grass	Tall grass with long, arching leaves
Onopordum acanthium Cotton thistle	Grey spiny leaves and round, purple, thistle-like flowers
Phormium tenax 'Sundowner' New Zealand flax	Fans of tall linear leaves striped dark green and pink
Phyllostachys nigra Black bamboo	Tall upright stems mature to a dark brown or black; dramatic plant for lighting
Prunus laurocerasus 'Otto Luyken' Cherry laurel	Cultivar with large, shiny, evergreen leaves and clusters of white flowers in spring
Prunus lusitanica Portuguese laurel	Red stems and dark evergreen leaves; the cultivar *P. l.* 'Variegata' has green and white leaves and is even more effective
Rheum palmatum Ornamental rhubarb	Very large, coarsely toothed leaves which are green above and purple-red beneath
Rhus typhina 'Dissecta' Cutleaf staghorn sumach	Gently contorted stems that bear dissected leaves which turn brilliant scarlet in autumn
Rosa moyesii	Arching stems of pink roses in midsummer, followed by large, flask-shaped, red hips
Rubus biflorus	Conspicuous white stems in winter
Salix exigua Coyote willow	Fine silvery foliage – one of the best grey-leaved plants for lighting
Sambucus nigra f. *laciniata* Fern-leafed elder	A lovely elder with finely cut, green leaves
Sambucus racemosa 'Plumosa Aurea' Red-berried elder	Golden, serrated leaves and red berries
Sisyrinchium striatum 'Aunt May'	Clumps of evergreen, green and cream, iris-like foliage
Verbascum olympicum Mullein	The tall spikes of grey-white, woolly leaves topped with bright yellow flowers
Viburnum plicatum 'Mariesii'	Tiered branches with pendulous leaves and erect white flowers
Yucca filamentosa Adam's needle	Sharply pointed, sword-like, evergreen leaves

interpreted sensitively and the lighting carefully placed if the subject is to be attractively illuminated. A figure of a woman turning shyly to the left will be emphasized if it is lit mainly from the right, while a boldly striding or running figure must be lit strongly to emphasize the line and outline that convey this movement. The face must be illuminated appropriately, with subtlety for a shy, upward glance and with boldness, possibly including deep shadow, for a strong male figure or animal sculpture, such as a lion. An upward-facing figure seeking inspiration from the sky will not be enhanced by uplighting from below, which will merely emphasize the chin below the unlit face and features. The intensity of light and its direction will intensify movement and expression only if we can appreciate the viewing angle – lighting a face for frontal expression is pointless if the statue is subsequently positioned to gaze in profile towards a further vista.

above: This brightly lit statue is the centre of attention, the exotic planting has been lit less brightly, so as not to detract from it.

right: Uplighting this bust of Brutus against the dark niche in the hedge behind illustrates the importance of contrasting light and darkness in emphasising drama in focal points.

Statues and focal points

Statues and focal points need to be brightly lit if they are to fulfil their role as centres of attention. If there are several focal points in a view, they need not be illuminated equally – some should be treated as having secondary or tertiary importance and be lit less brightly. A pair of urns flanking a view through to a statue beyond should be lit less brightly than the statue, which is the primary focus. Moreover, because the statue is farther away, it will need to be more brightly lit than the closer urns. For example, if the statue were at the same approximate distance as the urns, lighting the urns with 20-watt lamps and the statue with a 35-watt lamp would establish the primacy of the statue within the view. If the statue were further away than the urns, trading up to a 50-watt lamp would preserve its dominance.

Lighting statues

A statue is a very individual statement in a garden. It is a reflection of the owner's personal taste, so its character must be

Locating statues

The site of the statue will also determine the lighting scheme, both in its brightness relative to other statues or focal points and in relation to its surroundings. A classical warrior posed in front of a hedge is like an actor on a stage, so additional lighting behind the statue or to either side, to wash the hedge, will provide the appropriate theatrical backdrop. This will also help to avoid lumpy shadows being projected onto the hedge. On the other hand, a running figure or animal sculpture may be pictured as running out of a dark void for strong contrast with the darkness behind, which will emphasize drama and movement. A statue may also be tucked away in a corner as a surprise for the evening stroller, and the lighting can reflect its surreptitious or mischievous presence.

Bulky plinths can get in the way of good lighting, but sometimes recessed uplights can be engineered into large plinths, provided that it is considered when the lighting circuits and statue are first planned. Remember to throw a little light on to the plinth itself so that the statue does not appear to be airborne in darkness, unless that is the specific intention, for a subject such as a flying bird or mythological figure.

Other focal points

Other types of focal points share many of the same characteristics as statues when it comes to lighting, whether they are urns, troughs, armillary spheres, sundials or obelisks. Water features,

above: The Buddha at the top of the water staircase is lit for prominence in the view.

COMPARATIVE POWER OF LIGHTING REQUIRED TO COMPENSATE FOR DISTANCE FROM VIEWPOINT (TUNGSTEN HALOGEN LAMPS)

A statue that is situated at some distance from the viewpoint must be lit more brightly than one that is situated close to the window or patio from which it is mainly observed in order to achieve the same impact.

15m	10m	5m	2m	**DISTANCE**
75 watts	50 watts	35 watts	20 watts	**LAMP POWER**

decorative panels in walls and paving and some garden structures are, of course, also focal points, and the same rules relating to distance from viewpoint and establishing a hierarchy apply to them. Ornamental benches can be difficult, because lighting them as focal points may result in glare that will be uncomfortable for anyone sitting there. Downlighting from a structure or tree is the best solution if such mounting points are available.

Colour and lighting intensity

The intensity of lighting required depends on colour as much as on the distance of the subject from the viewpoint, or its brightness relative to the background and other focal points. The high reflectance of a white marble subject makes a low lighting intensity necessary, otherwise it may be over-lit, producing a bright white glow instead of subtle shadows. On the other hand, dark bronze statues have a very low reflectance and will need fairly bright lighting if they are to stand out as focal points from any distance. The problem with bronze is that it is often shiny, and, if you light it with a few beams of very high-intensity lighting, you will be rewarded by a high-intensity shine. The

trick with bronze statues is to use a larger number of lower-power sources, each directed towards a separate part of the statue selectively but with sufficient overlap to make the lighting effect look complete. This may involve using narrower-beam spotlights to emphasize facial expression, muscular tone or particular ornament, while filling in other parts with a wash of light from wider-beam spotlights.

Other colour challenges will present themselves in planning lighting effects. Light statues on dark plinths will stand out well while the plinth remains of secondary importance, but in the reverse situation you may struggle to focus enough light on a dark subject for it to stand out without stray light emphasizing the lightness of the plinth. Sometimes the simplest answer is to encourage the lighter stone plinth to weather so that the balance is correct even in daylight.

Uplighting statues

Uplighting from directly in front of a statue or focal point can produce a washed out, two-dimensional effect (especially for a light-coloured subject). Close uplighting can project strong shadows onto the upper part of a figure

above: Uplighting would have resulted in a dark equine face above a bright plinth. Moonlighting from a tree provides a dappled, less dramatic lighting effect, which also provides background from the pampas grass.

below: The light coloured statue and white tulips are highly reflective with relatively low power lighting. Gentle uplighting and moonlighting of the avenue of apple trees behind adds depth to the view.

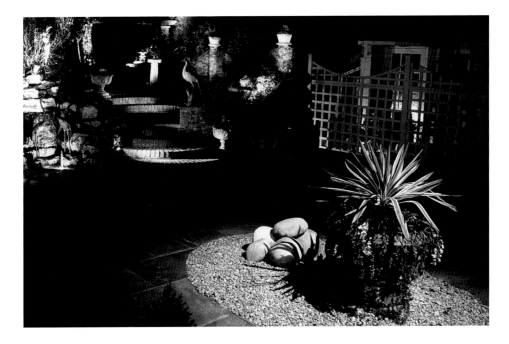

from protrusions at a lower level. Such shadows give a sense of menace to a face, as any fan of vintage horror movies knows, and occasionally this is useful for exaggerating facial expression.

If, however, it is a figure with arms akimbo or holding an object below face level, the face may be totally hidden. The answer is to position the luminaire back about 50cm (20in) from the base of the statue to give the light beam a chance to light the planes of the face, neck and shoulders. An uplight placed slightly to one side of the viewing axis will highlight form and relief with contrasting light and subtle shadow for a fuller effect, avoiding the cardboard cut-out effect of frontal lighting. Spike-mount spotlights are easily moved to customize the effect on installation, but recessed uplights may need to be set in concrete niches in paving before the statue reaches the site, so no adjustment is possible apart from that available by tilting the lamp cradle within the recessed body.

Crosslighting statues

Lighting from one side only can leave a statue looking curiously lopsided, so consider crosslighting from two opposing directions, using lighting of different intensities to achieve crosslit shadow while maintaining all-round illumination. This can be achieved either by changing the lamp on one side to a lower wattage or having a different beam spread to diffuse the light. Alternatively, moving one spotlight 1m (3ft) further away can be enough to make the difference. Spike-mount spotlights hidden in the edge of planted areas are convenient and flexible, although crosslighting may also be achieved with surface-mounted spotlights mounted on a wall, pergola or tree. Downlighting from these same positions may be the answer for some upward-facing statues, those on large plinths or planted containers, in which the plant might be hidden from uplighting by the lip of the jardinière. In practice, many features benefit from a combination of uplighting, downlighting and crosslighting. Sometimes, accent lighting from one source makes a feature stand out, while infill lighting adds a diffuse element to soften hard shadows or a stark scene. While simple uni-directional lighting will add drama to a subject, the addition of an extra dimension is worthwhile. For example, a phormium in an attractive urn can be downlit, while a soft uplight will show the form of the container.

above: Spotlighting onto the phormium from the house wall highlights the architectural leaf form while casting shadow within the pool of light framing the gravel oval. This is a perfect illustration of fitting the oval pool of light to the shape on the ground.

left: Grazing up the house wall emphasizes the texture, as well as the colour of the brickwork, while also silhouetting the magnolia tree. The whole view is reflected in a rectangular pond to be enjoyed from the temple, (see page 61).

Structures

Architectural lighting techniques may also apply to features and backdrops around the garden. Outbuildings designed to relate to the architectural features of the home should be lit to match, whether as an accompaniment to a path, a backdrop to a statue, an invitation to other areas such as a guesthouse or pool area, or as features in their own right.

Follies

Some buildings may merely be follies built as focal points rather than functional structures, while decorative façades or false doorways can ornament purely functional buildings. Many ideas fundamental to architectural lighting are described on pages 41–4, it just needs a little imagination to recognize features of architectural merit and to apply appropriate techniques. Of course, free-standing arches and other structures built as perspective and decorative devices are also an invitation to experiment with lighting skills. An arch, for example, may be used to divide two areas. Consider uplighting, to draw attention to it as the threshold to another outdoor room, or to frame the view through it to a focal point.

Gazebos

Gazebos are built to provide a viewpoint over the garden as a whole or a particular scene or feature. Bear this in mind before lighting such features purely as focal points in their own right, because ornamental lighting of the structure must be carefully placed to avoid glare to people wandering in and taking a seat. Gentle uplighting or moonlighting is better than crosslighting, which is likely to be invasive within the structure.

Interior downlighting will avoid an 'unoccupied' feel and can be used to illuminate decorative floor detail, but remember that less is more, and keep it soft. The difference between mood lighting and lighting for reading can be important in these structures. It is essential to decide priorities at the outset. Downlighting in a gazebo that is bright enough to facilitate reading will not encourage anyone to sit there quietly to look out on ornamentally lit features. Options for alternative levels of lighting, including the ability to switch off interior downlighting, should be provided.

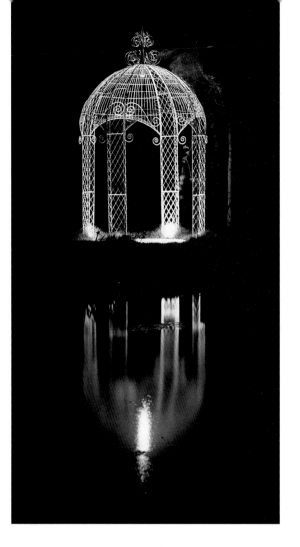

above: Four 20 watt uplights make this Victorian wirework gazebo stand out in the darkness and allow reflection in the water in the foreground. A small white 20 watt downlight at the apex illuminates mozaic tiling below.

ARCHITECTURAL LIGHTING

ILLUMINATION CAN BE USED TO EMPHASIZE THE STRUCTURE AND DETAILS OF BUILDINGS IN THE GARDEN. SIMPLE IDEAS ARE OFTEN THE MOST EFFECTIVE.

- Recess downlights under a porch canopy to illuminate the front door and provide a focus for visitors
- Uplight buttresses or columns with narrow beams to emphasize their structure
- Introduce uplights between windows, using narrow- or medium-beam lamps, to illuminate the façade without causing glare indoors
- Uplight architectural planting to throw the shadows of branches and leaves onto blank walls
- Wash lighting down façades over porches or lower structures to reveal their shape distinctly from the main building
- Crosslight steps leading up to doors for safety and to emphasize the texture of the paving
- Use narrow-beam spotlights to emphasize unusual wall features, such as plaques, clocks or relief panels
- Use shielded luminaires to light window reveals and to emphasize interesting arches or cornices
- Use interior lighting to emphasize unusual glazed features, such as stained glass or unusually shaped windows
- Graze up brick or stone walls from near the base to emphasize their texture and colour

above: Uplighting the pergola columns also illuminates the wide-spreading branches of the tree and is complemented by downlighting from between the beams.

Pergolas

Pergolas can be illuminated by uplighting the climbing plants that are scrambling up the supporting piers, or by downlighting with luminaires on the crossbeams or the top of the posts or columns. A combination of the two approaches is often the best choice, but will depend on the function of the pergola. If it is primarily an ornamental feature or serves the function of an archway framing a view, uplighting will emphasize the structure and the material of which the uprights are built, as well as casting light across plants creeping along the crossbeams.

The power of the lighting required will be determined at least partly by the colour of the material, whether the evening sky or a dark area is behind it, and by its distance from the focal point. Narrow-beam 20- or 35-watt lamps in spike-mount or recessed uplights will generally be the right choice. It is usually a good idea to incorporate some element of gentle downlighting to bring the ground into the picture. Pergolas are often built as places to sit and possibly to dine, with associated focal points nearby. Such focal points then become the prime view and the pergola provides the ambience around and over the seating, while downlights mounted on the pergola or among adjacent planting illuminate the focal point.

Walkways

Where there is a seating area beneath a pergola or a path through it, you may want to consider downlighting as the dominant technique. For a walkway through a pergola, downlighting at the top of columns can show

right: 20-watt downlights in the top of the lattice columns provide a network of patterned light and shadow along the path. Spotlighting the statue at the end provides a focal point for strollers and from the terrace from which the path leads.

below: Small area lighting luminaires, featuring 20 watt halogen capsule lamps, are mounted on each upright to provide general lighting for sitting out and also an attractive wash of light which brings out the colour of the terracotta wall.

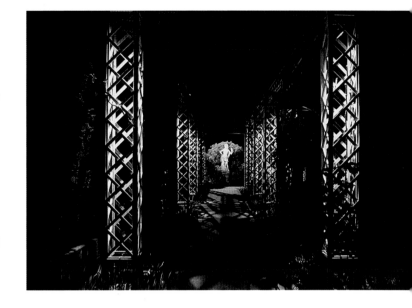

upward-facing flowers as well as casting the shadow of the climbing plants down onto the path. This can leave the crossbeams unlit. This may not be important if they are silhouetted against skyglow in a city, if there are no climbing plants growing across them, or if there is a focal point at the end of a pergola that is framed by the illuminated columns advancing towards it. Often, however, the best solution will be a combination of uplighting on the columns and downlighting from the crossbeams to provide path lighting beneath.

Dining areas

Where the pergola frames a dining area, downlighting can illuminate the table while uplighting casts light on the surrounding 'room' created by the shrub borders or climbing plants growing up the supporting columns or posts. If the pergola is small and huddles closely around the dining table, uplighting the nearby columns or posts will cause glare for anyone who happens to glance backwards. In a closely confined area it is preferable to use mainly downlighting with luminaires fitted with internal glare louvres or external glare guards, both

above: Uplighting from the planters projects shadows onto the walls while downlights provide illumination over the seating area. Sails and canopies can be used to diffuse and reflect light.

right: Ornamental lighting provides the ambience of this out-door room. Candles on the table provide a mellow contrast to electric lighting.

over the table and down the adjacent posts to light the surroundings of the posts and dining chairs. If the pergola has a large tree nearby, moonlighting down can add a romantic touch with its subtle effect, throwing gentle light and the shadow of beams and climbers onto the table below. Even then, do not forget to put candles on the table for a final touch of intimacy. Remember that if directional lighting is used close to areas that people use, luminaires with glare-control features must be used. The lighting must be soft enough to create a pleasant ambience, and luminaires must be carefully positioned both to avoid

glare and to ensure that faces are not left in shadow. Lamps should be 20 watts, at most 35 watts, with wide beams.

Area lighting

Area lighting products are sometimes used for illuminating pergola areas, and although some small luminaires make an unobtrusive contribution towards the ambience of a dining area under a pergola, larger ones can be over-bright and draw the eye away from the scene. Halogen capsule lamps can be contained within small luminaires located between the beams or colour-matched to the posts or columns to be unobtrusive.

Hanging lanterns are often a hazard to taller visitors. Luminaires designed for the walls of the house should not clutter a decorative structure or provide obstacles at head height to bump into. Using such unsuitable lighting products in such contexts looks wrong unless the fittings match a design theme, such as oriental brass lanterns in a pergola or gazebo designed for an Eastern effect.

You must think ahead if you wish to avoid a clutter of visible wiring running up a stone column or brick pier. A conduit within the structure provides cable-ways from the ground up to the pergola beams and is an unobtrusive way of achieving this. Metal structures often feature hollow tubing through which wiring can be threaded. Cable channels can be routed in timber posts so that wiring can be hidden under matching trim pieces prepared at the same time as the posts.

Steps

Lighting steps for safety is an obvious requirement in a garden, but it can also be decorative. Using downlighting from adjacent lighting platforms is often the best way; downlighting from an adjacent wall can produce step- and pathlighting accompanied by grazing of attractive brickwork, while moonlighting from a tree can give a natural effect in a country garden. One of the newer techniques is based on the linear lighting techniques described earlier. It consists of running a linear lighting source in a channel under the nosing of the step or fixing a moulding or metal extrusion that provides the fixing for the light source as well as shielding it from view as you ascend the steps. It is a stylish approach, but it tends to produce a fairly bright effect because such products are generally developed for commercial and public premises. It is also moderately expensive for domestic use.

left: Recessed bricklights illuminate the path while stem-mounted luminaires light the steps upwards. Some uplighting of small trees adds interest.

right: Linear lighting in an aluminium extrusion under the nosing of the steps provides bright and distinctive staircase lighting.

Steplights

If overhead lighting cannot be installed and linear lighting would be too expensive, crosslighting the steps from the flanking walls is one of the best techniques for lighting steps. Recessed steplights, normally using 20-watt dichroic reflector lamps to project beams across a staircase, graze across the treads to display texture and colour and to light them for access.

Steplighting should be as uniform as possible, lighting both risers and treads to avoid shadowing from one step onto the next. On an extended staircase, there should be no glare directed downwards towards the eyes of the ascending pedestrian. The key to fulfilling these requirements without using blander area lighting techniques is to use more luminaires, each one lighting across two, or at most three, steps. Using wider-beam, higher-brightness lamps may keep the cost down, but it will provide poor uniformity, with dangerous shadow and increased glare. Wider staircases may be lit by using narrower-beam lamps to project further across the steps but be careful to guard against glare.

Most steplights are essentially recessed spotlights. You may need to use internal glare louvres or products

LINEAR LIGHTING FOR STEPS

The aluminium extrusion is fixed under the stair nosing. A linear 'lightstring' fitted with long-life lamps is installed in the channel, wired to a remote low-voltage transformer and covered with a protective clear polycarbonate cover.

with shielding grills or eyelid hoods. Make sure that any steplight facing a terrace, path, window or other viewpoint is of a low-glare type, using a capsule lamp rather than a spotlight-type lamp. Such products are sometimes designed for surface-mounting and are fairly small because they contain only a small capsule lamp and do not have to cater for a larger reflector lamp. These can be installed where it is not possible or desirable to bore holes in the walls. Another option is a bricklight flushed into the wall. These area lighting products provide a subtle light and will avoid the directional glare of a spotlight. A bricklight with an opal lens but without a louvred front may still appear as a bit of a 'hotspot', while louvres to prevent glare will cut out half of the light and limit spread to a smaller semicircle, which, in turn, requires more luminaires.

Spreadlights for steps

Where there is no flanking wall, it is best to diffuse light from the side. Some surface-mounted steplights are available on spike-mounting stems so that they can be tucked into hedges and adjacent planting to provide a small pool of light for two or three narrow steps. For wider steps, a wider

pool of light is required, but it is a good idea to have a hood over the light source to conceal the lamp. This is how the spreadlight, or 'mushroom light' as many consumers think of it, was born. Selecting a spreadlight that will stand up high enough to perform its lighting job yet still be visually acceptable is the necessary trade-off. Typical spreadlights use a tungsten or halogen lamp of about 20 watts and provide a circle of coverage of 2–2.5m (6–8ft) diameter for a light 30cm (1ft) tall, increasing to a 3.5–4m (11–13ft) circle for one 60cm (2ft) tall.

Paths

The same considerations and design techniques discussed for steps (see pages 91–2) also apply to paths, although the length of the path is likely to be greater than the width of the steps, so the emphasis is on the spread of light. This means that brick lights and spreadlights will be the preferred fittings, although down-lighting and moonlighting will be the preferred decorative techniques. Where the path is wide or the circulation area is a larger one, area lighting techniques, as applied in some cases to drives, may come into play.

below: Steplights hidden under treads light some steps directly and others by reflecting the light around the area from surrounding walls.

above: A downlight on the arch and spreadlights in adjacent borders provide effective pathlighting. Uplighting of planting provides a sense of space and security along the route.

garden while they enjoy each other's company and the garden features. In a formal garden layout we would expect to see regular lighting patterns, but in an informal setting too much regularity can destroy the atmosphere. As long as there is enough lighting to enable a person to walk along the path without having to think too consciously about it, they can also enjoy illuminated features along the way. It does not matter if the layout is not strictly spaced or if luminaires are paired along either side of the path or staggered on either side. As long as the pools of light from the various sources overlap, or nearly so, then it will be uniform enough.

Driveways

Lighting driveways is usually a compromise between providing good lighting and keeping the light sources invisible, but this is not always possible. Moonlighting from trees is an attractive way of lighting a horizontal surface in a natural way that is suitable for both town and country gardens. However, if there are no trees, walls or structures to act as lighting platforms, the light fittings are bound to be visible. Area lighting on walls, or lanterns perched on gate pillars, will provide lighting that is mainly for orientation purposes – that is, giving enough light to see by, to find the way, to fetch and carry objects, to perform simple tasks, such as finding a key.

Lighting planting and features adjacent to the driveway certainly marks the route, but some lighting will usually be needed for pedestrians to use the road. Around driveways, as well as wide paths and open access areas for parking, bollard lights, which project more outward light than spreadlights, will give broader coverage but there will be some increased visibility of the light sources. Small halogen bollards are often popular because of their size, and some models are available in modern shapes and fashionable finishes such as copper and stainless steel. For practical purposes around a driveway, particularly around parking or turning areas, taller

The fundamental difference between lighting a level route and lighting changes of level: people are accustomed to walking along a level surface and need less lighting than for negotiating steps, unless there are obstacles, such as children's toys, lying around. Lighting focal points and adjacent planting for a reassuring ambience also serves to waymark the route, so in most gardens pathlighting does not need to be as bright or uniform as steplighting. Indeed, it can be a useful means of avoiding the 'runway' effect of regularly spaced luminaires along a straight path.

Regular spacing of lighting helps to make sure that the eye does not have to try to adapt too frequently to different lighting intensities, which can cause disorientation. However, a path in a garden is usually a meandering, pedestrian route that is intended to allow friends and family to move around a mains-voltage bollard lights with higher power light sources are required. Column-mounted lanterns – either real or scaled-down street lights – will always be a popular choice with traditionalists or for lighting on a grand scale, but they are used as daytime ornaments as much as working night-time light sources.

Patios and terraces

There is a large number of possible lighting combinations, but for large patio areas different combinations of wall luminaires and low-power floodlights under the eaves will be required for different functions. Brighter lighting may be necessary when you have to keep an eye on children, whereas something a little less bright would be appropriate for gatherings of adults. Provided this is done with taste and restraint, it can create a satisfactory compromise between mood lighting and the higher light levels needed for activity and security. For smaller, more intimate areas, a more subtle approach is needed. Moonlighting is again the most suitable lighting technique for horizontal areas and atmospheric spaces, but there is not always a large enough tree close by, especially where the patio is immediately outside the house, to provide the necessary support.

Downlighting

Downlighting from below the eaves of a house can be an effective way of lighting paths, terraces and planting around the house to create a welcoming atmosphere. It can also produce a grazing effect if the lighting of a surface from an oblique angle emphasizes texture, such as roughness in brick or stone and the patterns of the mortar joints. This effect can also be produced by placing uplights close to the base of a wall to create a feeling of warmth and intimacy around a terrace.

Downlights and wall-mount spots should be discreet and match the mounting surface or other external fittings as closely as possible. Glare guards or internal honeycomb louvres are often useful for a soft lighting effect and limiting glare. Recessing weather-proof downlights into the soffit below the eaves can be especially neat. Where structures exist over or next to the area

below: Downlights mounted under the eaves above the door make focal points of the urn, viewed from the inside of the house and also the entrance when viewed from the outside.

below: 'City moonlighting' is a term sometimes used for this method of lighting a roof garden. Wall mount spotlights shine down through container planting to cast the shadow of stem and foliage onto the decking, as well as to make a feature of the planting when viewed from inside.

where you require lighting, use ideas for lighting pergola areas (see pages 88–91). Lighting patios often requires a combination of downlights and products that will provide softer area lighting, and uplights to add contrast and emphasis, by uplighting individual features as well as balustrades, trellises or walls.

Area lighting

Wall-mounted lights on the house provide light for a patio area immediately outside French windows or a kitchen door and are the most familiar form of exterior lighting. They generally do a good job in providing the lighting needed for orientation and the performance of general tasks. Luminaires mounted at, or just above head height, provide lighting for everything below eye level and may cast some decorative light on the wall on which they are mounted, as well as any adjacent planting. At night the lights will draw as much attention to themselves as they do to the area they are intended to light, and for this reason it is important that the style should suit the house and that the lamps that are fitted are not of excessively high wattage. A wider area of illumination is worthless if

it is at the cost of being made to feel uncomfortable because of the glare.

While such lighting is not directional like a spotlight beam is, the light produced still has a direction of travel and will produce shadows. Anyone seated with their back to the wall light will see the faces of people seated opposite, but their own faces will be in shadow unless additional lighting has been provided from another direction. Good patio illumination, for dining especially, should be all-enveloping while preserving the view of the illuminated garden or landscape view. It should be wired by means of a separate switch so that the view out from the house is not inhibited by bright area lighting on the patio just outside the windows.

Barbecues

If you are going to dine outside, the chances are that you may also be cooking there. As with a dinner party indoors, you will want to leave the preparation and cooking areas out of sight once the meal is served. This is a simple matter of having one or more lights near the barbecue that can be switched off separately from the

ILLUMINATING A BARBECUE	
TYPE OF BARBECUE	**SUITABLE LIGHTING**
Free-standing barbecue against a wall	Spotlighting down onto barbecue or area lighting fixed to wall above
Free-standing barbecue under a pergola	Spotlights fixed to overhead beams
Free-standing barbecue near a tree	Spotlight fixed to tree by means of mounting bracket
Free-standing barbecue in open area	Post-mounted lantern or portable light on nearby table
Barbecue with brick or stone surround	Post-mounted accent light or spreadlight on surface mount
Barbecue with raised brick or stone surround	Bricklights or steplights set into walls at either side

ornamental lighting and the lighting over or around the exterior dining table. The switch for the barbecue lighting should preferably be a weatherproof one near the barbecue.

Courtyards

In a small space around a dining area, consider gentle uplighting to reveal the shape of the space and the presence of planting to create an intimate feeling that contrasts with the indoor ambience. Uplighting can also throw the shadow of climbing plants upwards onto a rendered wall for added interest. This is particularly appropriate for courtyards, which are often shady places during the day but have walls that offer opportunities for creating a subtle and romantic ambience in the evening. Walls with interesting stone or brickwork can be grazed by uplights or downlights to emphasize the texture, the colour of the material and the shape of the walled enclosure. Low-power downlighting can throw the foliage shadow onto the paving below in an imaginative miniaturization of the moonlighting effect seen with trees.

Balconies and roof terraces

Lofty terraces on the top or side of buildings have a magic of their own at night: their dizzy height commands a view and it is the job of lighting to reinforce this, not negate it by lighting the space only for its own sake. Lighting should be secondary to the view and consist mainly of low-level lighting across the decking or paving, accepting the wash of interior lighting through picture windows and so easing the transition from interior to exterior. Overhead lighting, if suitable mounting points exist, can perform two functions. First, it should add downlighting for key plants or features; and second, it should provide lighting for dining or reading. Both types of lighting should be wired on separate switches so that brighter lighting can be switched off to allow the vista beyond to be seen more clearly. Any ornamental lighting, whether it is downlighting or uplighting, must be discreet and concentrate merely on framing the view and contributing a pleasant ambience.

above left: The arched trellis feature is lit so that it can be seen through the arch from the seating area in the foreground. The priority is to draw the eye down into the roof garden and away from the surrounding buildings.

Lighting design for the outdoor room

above: The uplighting of the bamboo, shrubs and rock water feature frames the decking and seating area. Spotlights under the plank bridge light the cobbled stream bed.

In an integrated garden design, remembering what not to light and by how much is as important as remembering what to light; a good design will exploit the potential of shadow to create depth and perspective. Although every garden is different, some general guidelines can be applied to creating lighting plans, which can be adapted to suit different types of garden. The ideas and examples will help you devise a plan for your own garden.

Editing the view

If you do not light it, you will not see it. Observing this rule for compost heaps, outbuildings and utility areas may seem obvious and, although lighting for access to these areas may be required for functional reasons, the lights should be on separate circuits so that they can be switched on separately from the ornamental garden lighting. It is also important to consider this rule when you are placing luminaires so that they are carefully directed only at the objects you wish to light and not at the children's climbing frame or other background areas that do not contribute to the ornamental view.

In newly planted gardens, the small size of the initial planting is likely to limit the amount of lighting installed in the first year, unless there are attractive walls or trellis to stand in as lighting subjects while the plants develop. Unless you are installing an entire system in one go, first-year installation may be limited to areas of hard landscaping, focal points, structures and any existing mature specimen plants. To attempt more can often result in nothing more than a well-lit fence.

The scope for adding luminaires as planting matures should have been planned at the beginning. Avoid over-lighting by illuminating every shrub and paving stone. As with so many things, less is more.

Inside looking out

When you have installed garden lighting, a window ceases to be something to be covered with blinds when dusk falls. Instead it becomes a frame for the picture of the illuminated garden. However this only works if the balance of interior and exterior lighting is correct. Insufficient outdoor light results in the 'black mirror' effect – you see your own reflection and that of the room around you in the dark glass of the window. If the primary objective is to enjoy the view from the house, the exterior lighting must be brighter than the interior lighting so the 'black mirror' will become transparent glass and allow the view through. This is also a matter of making sure that the interior lighting is not too bright or, perhaps, that it can be dimmed according to mood so that the garden illumination becomes more visible. Nowhere is this

above: The wall fountain provides a focal point to look at from inside the house as well as within the courtyard itself.

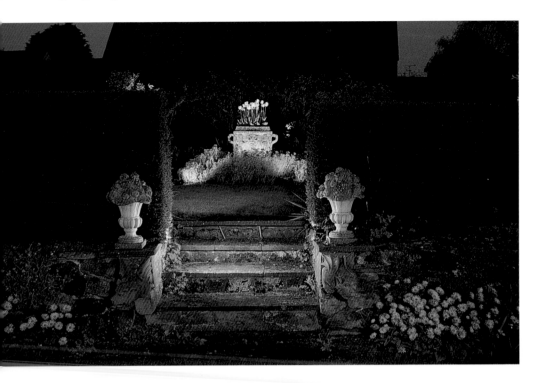

above: Crosslighting the steps from luminaires tucked under the bottom of the hedge also lights the route through to the next 'room'. The steps lead the eye through to the illuminated planter beyond, while the urns frame the view. Foreground illumination is provided by area lighting on the house walls.

more important than in a conservatory where almost the whole room can become a black mirror. In a conservatory, 'point' sources of light, such as chandeliers, should be avoided because these are reflected brilliantly in every pane of glass. Using discreet downlighting by surface- or track-mounted spotlights or wire-lighting systems onto interior features and seating areas can produce better results. If a chandelier or decorative lantern is used over a dining table it should be connected to a separate switch so that it can be removed from the view when not needed.

Setting lighting priorities

Lighting selectively should not depend on random choice. It must be based on establishing a sense of priority within the view. Once the viewpoints are established from windows, as well as from the the patio and seats around the garden, each view must have a balanced composition. It is essential to decide on the primary focal point within a view (see pages 82–5), because a pair of objects demanding equal attention can confuse the eye. If there are several important features, perhaps a group of figures, for example, either light them as

a group or establish a hierarchy between them so that the primary focal point is most brightly lit, while features of secondary or tertiary importance are less so.

Make it easy on the eye

Although we praise the notion of contrasting light and shadow, it is important to remember the difference between shadow and darkness. Shadow is created by light, whereas darkness is the result of an absence of light. Leaving some areas in darkness may be a creative decision so that illuminated objects in the foreground stand out, or so that a vista is maintained if there is a view of a city or landscape from a balcony or roof garden. It may be a result of a fall of the ground if there is no backdrop to light behind the statue or tree and we must be content with the sunset sky or the glitter of stars for our background. There is always a danger of being too selective, either because of a conscious decision to light only one or two features or a lack of awareness of the resulting starkness.

Most subjects benefit from being given a sense of place in the garden, especially by having a background of a hedge, wall or planting illuminated at a lower level. It is important to provide a link between focal points so that the eye is not continually adapting to brightness and darkness as it pans across the scene. Lighting shrub borders is one of the main ways of achieving this in the vertical plane, but if the horizontal plane is also lit it will add the third dimension to the view. Moonlighting onto a lawn or introducing some simple spreadlighting of a path are ways of achieving this.

Emphasizing depth

Ideas for emphasizing depth and providing a link within the view are always worth considering, but they assume an added importance when we consider perspective, which can appear quite different in artificial lighting compared with daylight conditions. Lighting a statue more brightly will make it appear closer to the viewer, but it will recede further into the view if it is less brightly lit.

The choice of lighting brightness depends partly on the relative importance attributed to the features, but also on its distance from the viewpoint. A small statue placed near the edge of the patio close to the house may well be over-lit by anything more powerful than a 20-watt lamp. If the same statue were placed three times as far

away, you would almost certainly need to use a 35-watt or even a 50-watt lamp. Bear in mind that a small statue may be too tiny to be seen from the house, in daylight or at night if it is too far away, and it will therefore lose its role as a focal point. Replacing it with a larger subject at the same distance from the house may require two or more lamps of 50 watts or more. No matter how brightly we light a subject in relation to its distance from the viewpoint, lighting a distant subject should be avoided if it is not to appear to float in blackness. Aim to achieve a blend between a brighter focal point and a less bright middle ground consisting of a little light cast on the lawn and illumination of shrub borders on either side. Lighting flanking shrub borders will visually 'push' the sides of the garden view outwards to make the space feel larger and avoid the tunnel vision that is associated with a single illuminated focal point.

Front gardens

Front gardens are often neglected areas as far as ornamental lighting is concerned. While paths, steps and drives usually receive lighting treatment of some kind and lighting around the front door is almost universal, decorating our home does not often extend to having a

below: Uplighting of the tree and formal features provides an attractive front garden scene when the visitor ascends the illuminated steps.

front-garden lighting scheme. Lighting decorative features helps to put the home in the context of its plot and to put the paths and steps in the context of the space they cross. Lighting may need to be protected from vandals by being recessed into the ground, but otherwise there is no reason not to use all the ornamental lighting techniques possible for other areas. The illumination may be a little more low key than in rear-garden areas, and some home-owners may prefer to have it wired to a separate switch from drive or house wall lights, so it can be used more selectively.

Preserving a vista

If the balanced view we have achieved between distant focal point, background and middle ground is to be appreciated, the foreground lighting must be subtle and subdued if we are to see beyond it to the more distant panorama. Leaving the foreground unlit can distort the perspective, however, because the outer view will appear closer than it really is. Gentle, low-level lighting of foreground features, such as urns, architectural planting or the low branches of a tree near the patio, will frame the view and maintain perspective. This is particularly important where the distant view is just that – distant.

One situation in which garden lighting, whether ornamental or practical, will be secondary to anything else is the balcony, roof garden or hillside terrace with a city view or perhaps a seascape. In these locations, the view outward will have priority and any artificial lighting within the area will have only a supporting role. The task here is to preserve the view, which may be achieved by framing it through subtle lighting of plants or structures, or by introducing lighting within the space to cater for eating and entertaining but that can be controlled at will, with separate switches for different lighting functions and moods. The same applies in larger gardens where you wish to see the illuminated garden rather than any brightly lit areas near the house or viewpoint. Switching off area lighting close to you will enable you to see the view beyond the patio.

Outdoor rooms

These days, gardens are often divided into several 'rooms', which are separate from each other, may have different uses and may or may not be directly visible from the house or patio. If there is a swimming pool, for example, we do not necessarily want to see the area around it when we look out of a window.

When there are several rooms within a single garden, individual vistas may appear differently according to the part of the garden from which they are seen, or a view may be seen unexpectedly as you walk from one part of the garden to another. The lighting scheme might, therefore, have to include separate switches for lighting within each garden room while at the same time taking account of the layout of the overall garden and the need to provide lighting for access

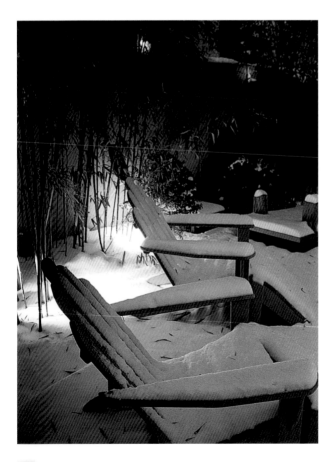

below: Switching on the garden lighting after a snowfall can create a seasonal surprise.

between the different rooms within the garden. There are occasions, however, when multiple viewpoints will not make any difference to the controls: a front garden should be attractively lit whether someone is entering or leaving the house or simply looking at it through a window.

Creating flexibility

For every type of garden activity, there are a host of personal variations. Just as the design of the garden itself is determined by the style of the house and the personality of the owner, the lighting scheme will be similarly affected. In addition, the lighting must take into account the lifestyle of the homeowner and reflect constraints imposed by the seasons. For example, it may be important to be able to light the garden for both large parties and intimate gatherings. Someone with a large garden might even want a scheme that allows a range of activities to be carried out in different parts of the garden at the same time. Lighting

must also be flexible enough to suit the mood of the occasion. At the end of a meal, for instance, being able to direct light towards a table is less important than lighting the view from the patio.

Seasonal changes may necessitate alterations in the way that lighting is used. Some people will want a lighting scheme that allows them to look over the garden from a conservatory or sitting room in winter, or makes barbecues more enjoyable in summer. In winter there is no need to light the herbaceous borders, which will have died down. Moonlighting can look stark when the leaves that provided the dappled shadows have fallen, and underwater lighting will not be needed when the pump has been switched off. Although these may seem obvious points, they are easily overlooked, so that the extra switch or cable needed is omitted from the original plan. Considering every potential use of the garden at every time of the year will ensure the lighting scheme is useful all year round.

above: In winter the dead stems used by flower arrangers can be left, instead of being cut down, to complement evergreen planting and the bare skeletons of deciduous trees. This view from a conservatory is preferable to the 'black mirror' effect.

Choosing products

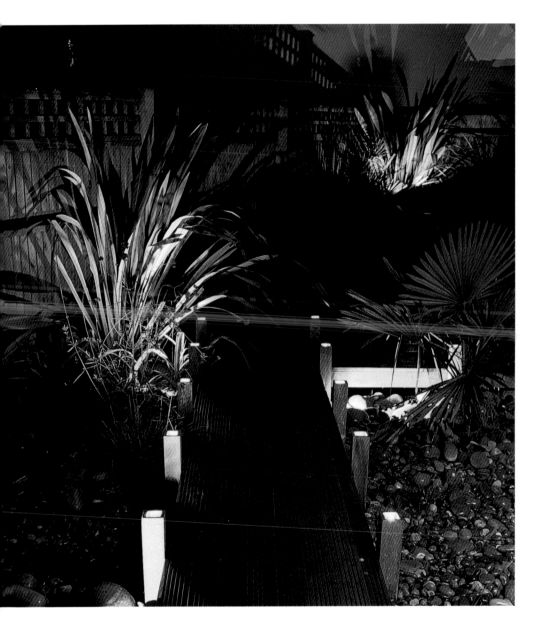

above: Lighting effects are all the more intriguing when lights are hidden below decking, behind landscape features or recessed in the ground. The onlooker's pleasure is heightened by curiosity about how the effects are achieved.

Choosing the luminaires that will meet the needs identified in your plan is the last step in developing a lighting scheme. The models you select should be attractive where viable, but in most cases you will look for those that are unobtrusive: they may be small, coloured to blend in with their surroundings or recessed, or they may have all three characteristics. In addition, you will want to select products that are reliable and easy to maintain.

Weatherproof or waterproof?

The first consideration is that the luminaires must be weatherproof or waterproof enough to perform their required functions. The two terms are not interchangeable. Lights for use underwater must be waterproof in the true sense of the word and keep the lamp and electrical parts dry even when the luminaire is submerged in water. Most lights, however, will not be used underwater, and it will suffice that they are weatherproof. In most cases, they should be rainproof – that is, proof against water spray from above – while others will have to be suitable for use where hosepipes and irrigation systems may result in water spray from the side or even from below. This does not always mean that water is totally excluded, merely that any water that enters has no harmful effects. Many wall lights and lanterns, for example, are constructed so that any water trickling in around the edge of glazing panels will run harmlessly out of the luminaire without touching any live electrical parts.

Dust and insects

The other elements that must be guarded against are solid ones. Dust blowing into a luminaire will necessitate more frequent cleaning, and nest-building by ants may result in a build-up of material that can cause a circuit breaker to trip out. It is also vital to protect small children, who may be tempted to experiment by poking objects into holes in a way that might have fatal results.

IP ratings

Luminaires are rated according to their resistance to the ingress of both liquids and solids by a code defining their Index of Protection – often known as an IP rating – which you will usually find in the product catalogue or specification. The letters IP are followed by two digits. The first of these quantifies protection against contact with live parts or ingress of solid bodies; the second indicates the level of protection against ingress of liquid. The box on page 106 provides a key to these figures and an explanation of their meaning. The figure 4 indicates the minimum standard acceptable for most exterior applications.

Many mains-voltage wall lights, column-mounted lanterns and bollard lights are rated from IP44 and include drainage holes to deal with any moisture that penetrates into the mounting. Some spike- and surface-mounted spotlights, especially those made from aluminium or copper spinnings, have a rating of IP54 or IP55. They rely on some degree of drainage because this method of construction makes it difficult to achieve a complete water seal.

below: Luminaires need to be more than rain-proof where pressure washers, hose pipes or irrigation systems are in use.

INDEX OF PROTECTION (IP) RATINGS

FIRST NUMERAL		SECOND NUMERAL	
NUMBER/ SYMBOL	DEGREE OF PROTECTION	NUMBER/ SYMBOL	DEGREE OF PROTECTION
4	(a) Protection against contact by tools, wires or the like, more than 1mm thick. (b) Protection against ingress of small foreign bodies.	4	Splash proof: liquid splashed from any direction shall have no harmful effect.
5	(a) Complete protection against contact. (b) Dustproof: protection against harmful deposits of dust; dust may enter but not in amount sufficient to interfere with satisfactory operation.	5	Jet proof: water projected by a nozzle from any direction (under stated conditions) shall have no harmful effect.
6	(a) Complete protection against contact. (b) Dust-tight: protection against ingress of dust.	6	Watertight equipment: protection against conditions on ship's decks, etc. Water from heavy seas or power jets shall not enter the enclosures under prescribed conditions.
IP CODE NOTES • Degree of protection is stated in form IPXX. • Protection against contact or ingress of water respectively is specified by replacing first or second X by digit number tabled, e.g. IP2X defines an enclosure giving protection against finger contact but without any specific protection against ingress of water or liquid. • Example:an underwater light should be rated at IP68. **Use this table for general guidance only.**		7	Protection against immersion in water: it shall not be possible for water to enter the enclosure under stated conditions of pressure and time.
		8	Protection against indefinite immersion in water under specified Pressure:it shall not be possible for water to enter the enclosure.

Spotlights made from aluminium or brass castings are usually machined and gasketed to achieve a rating of at least IP55, while lights to be recessed into walls or the ground need to be rated to at least IP56, so that they are proof against regular splashing or water spray. Underwater lights or recessed lights to be used in ground subject to waterlogging should be rated at IP68.

While these protection ratings are a good guide to a light's suitability for exterior use, they can realistically be achieved only when the equipment is correctly installed and used. Wall-mounted luminaires commonly require seals or sealants around fixing holes and cable entries, and these are usually specified in the instruction leaflets supplied by the manufacturers. Equally, underwater lights cannot be expected to retain a waterproof cable entry if they are dragged around a pond during weed clearance or other maintenance.

above: Recessed bricklights are a neat means of providing low level area lighting around a patio or along a path.

Surface or recessed lights?

Recessed uplights are often chosen because burying the luminaire in the ground seems the best way to uplight a subject without the light source being visible. Uplighting a tree growing out of a lawn with a flush recessed uplight will allow mowing to be carried out without the risk of damaging the luminaire or creating a trip hazard, which would occur with a spike-mounted uplight in the same place. In any open area, be it gravel, decking or paving, a neatly recessed luminaire will always be preferable for unobtrusive lighting. In other positions, however, a spike-mounted spotlight may be more flexible and less expensive, provided it can be hidden among low planting so it does not become a focal point in itself.

The same debate – surface or recessed – often arises with wall lights, especially low-level lighting used for steps. Recessed lights posi-tioned flush in a wall will always be less obtrusive than surface-mounted ones, and often the limited area – a small area of step, path or patio – means that the extra bulk of an adjustable luminaire is not acceptable. There are times, however, when fitting recessed lighting can be difficult or impossible, because wiring to the luminaires is not easy, but more often because the type of material used in wall construction will not permit it. This is sometimes the case with timber constructions when cutting holes would weaken the structure. Surface-mounted lights are, therefore, more commonly used in association with wooden decking.

above: This recessed metal halide uplight has an adjustable lampholder to allow the light beam to be focused in both direction and beam angle. A little condensation on the inside of the lens is common when the air trapped inside is humid and does no harm.

left: An adjustable, spike-mount copper spotlight is a compact and versatile unit to use at the front of a border where planting may not hide it completely.

SPOTLIGHTS VERSUS UPLIGHTS		
	ADVANTAGES	**DISADVANTAGES**
Spike-mounted spotlights	• Easily moved and focused • Adjustable head gives flexibility • Relatively inexpensive	• Obtrusive unless hidden by planting • Easily knocked out of position • Cabling susceptible to damage by dogs
Recessed uplights	• Unobtrusive in open areas • Can be mowed or swept over • Minimize trip hazard	• Only limited internal adjustment possible • More expensive than spike-mounted units • Easily covered by fallen leaves and other debris • Liable to internal condensation • Hot lenses can pose problems in paths or decks

right: The green finish of this small, halogen area light blends well with the painted timber around the patio and adjacent foliage.

Finishes and materials

The best garden lighting will be made from durable materials – aluminium, copper, brass and stainless steel. Such materials can dissipate heat so that luminaires do not overheat and cause premature lamp failure or distortion of the luminaire body. Good heat dissipation means lower lens and body temperatures, which is beneficial when there is accidental contact with the skin. Also luminaire designs can be smaller and less visually obtrusive.

The finish may be a natural one for some metals, which are used in bare or polished form, or an applied colour, which is usually a powder coat rather than a liquid paint finish, as a well-applied powder coat is much more durable. Some less expensive products may not have been properly prepared before powder-coating, and the powder coat sometimes peels off after a few years. As with everything, you get what you pay for. Different finishes are best suited to particular applications and locations and these are summarized opposite.

Selecting light fittings

For the most commonly used types of garden-lighting product there are a few key points that will make the lighting scheme more aesthetic or durable if the appropriate product choice is made. There are also a few 'tricks of the trade' for various product types and these are mentioned below.

Spike-mounted uplights and spotlights

Spike-mounted spotlights are the workhorses of most garden-lighting schemes because ground-mounted uplighting is the most common choice for lighting trees, shrubs, columns and focal points. Spike-mounted fixtures are the usual first choice because they

SELECTING FITTINGS FOR THE GARDEN

MATERIAL	COLOUR/FINISH	USES
Aluminium (powder coated)	Green	Spike-mounted spotlights blend with planting. Surface-mounted fittings blend with green-painted and -stained timber
	Black	Traditional finish matches architectural ironmongery, rose arches and so on. Often inexpensive
	White	Traditional finish matches architectural ironmongery, window frames conservatories and so on
	Customized colours	Sometimes available to special order so that luminaires blend or contrast with an existing scheme
	Silver/metal look	Inexpensive alternative to stainless steel for a modern look
Brass	Natural	Weathers to blend with light-coloured stone, gravel and pale timber. Polished brass will tarnish unless lacquered
Bronze	Natural	Weathers to a darker finish than brass
Chrome-plated	Polished	Decorative finish for modern settings
Copper	Natural	Weathered, mottled finish blends with timber, brick, gravel and bark mulch. Eventually weathers to verdigris
Stainless steel	Polished	Decorative finish for modern settings; durable in coastal locations

above: These luminaires could be matched to their surrounding: green amongst planting, black to match other hardware in the area, 'granite' in rockeries or 'antique copper' near red brick.

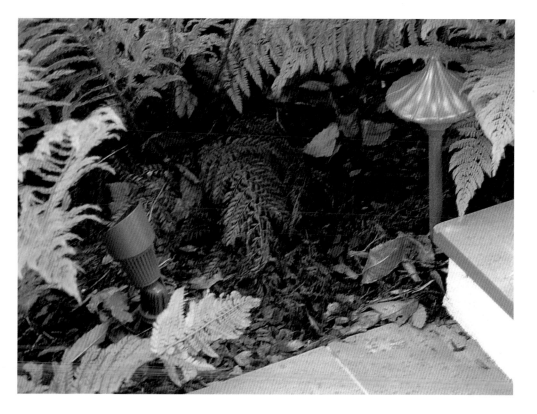

can be adjusted more than recessed fittings and are typically half the price.

Adjustable spotlights should have a bracket or knuckle, which can be locked in position with a screw or nut so they are less likely to be knocked out of focus. A ground spike with fins rather than just a tubular stem will help to prevent the spotlight from rotating in loose soil if the cable to it is disturbed (pegging down the cables leading to spotlights can also help to avoid such disturbance). A fitted glare guard is essential if the flexibility of spike-mounted spotlights is not to be limited near to paths or viewpoints, where glare can be a problem. Where a glare guard is not available or where its use would make the spotlight too bulky and visible, an internal 'honeycomb' louvre will help to shield the lamp from view. Similar criteria apply to the use of surface-mounted spotlights on walls, pergolas and trees.

Recessed uplights

Internal adjustability of the lamp housing is the main requirement if a recessed uplight is to be used to light one side of the vertical, so check that adjustability is possible – usually up to 15–20 degrees either side of vertical. Where the location is a route for pedestrians or traffic, a grid accessory over the top of the luminaire will prevent a foot from coming into contact with a hot lens or a stone stuck in the tread of a car tyre from puncturing the glass. Corrosion by ground salts can be a major problem with recessed uplights, particularly if the soil is especially acidic or alkaline. Brass luminaires are largely immune, and many higher-power luminaires are supplied with a plastic sleeve, which cradles the metal housing of the luminaire and holds it clear of the surrounding soil. It is usual to protect aluminium- and steel-bodied luminaires, even when they have been powder-coated or enamelled, by painting the recessed parts with a bituminous coating or adding a layer of washed sand around them when they are inserted into the ground. Drainage is also required under recessed lights to make sure they do not become waterlogged. Dig the hole recessed or surface-mounted, as it will make it easy to adjust them and replace the lamps in future years.

Spreadlights

This type of luminaire is highly visible in the garden because it needs to stand to a given height to spread a pool of light around it. Cast-aluminium alternatives are preferable where children are likely to test the strength of the fittings, and these are available in a variety of colours to blend with the background or to match other garden hardware. Copper spreadlights are particularly popular for their natural weathered appearance. Look for designs with a glass dome or tube to protect the lamp and its holder from irrigation or hosepipe spray. Some models are available with a choice of ground spike and surface mount. The latter is especially useful if you want to fix spreadlights around decking or the edge of planters, for example.

left: A brass underwater light, used without its usual fixing bracket and installed as a small recessed uplight, is hard to see amongst the pebbles surrounding the phormium.

below: A modern style in a traditional material: this small halogen bollard light weathers to an attractive brown patina, which blends well with brick and gravel and contrasts pleasantly with planting.

at least half as deep again as the luminaire's depth and fill the bottom with clean gravel before locating the luminaire in the ground. Do not use recessed uplights where regular waterlogging of the ground occurs unless they have an IP68 rating.

Underwater lights

All underwater lights, which must be rated at IP68 at least, should be equipped with a robust bracket with screw-locking adjustment so the luminaire's focus can be maintained even in swirling water. The luminaire will usually be fixed to an underwater block to anchor it in place, and all fixings must be either stainless steel or brass to be corrosion-proof. Most fixing screws used by manufacturers are stainless steel, and there may be a reaction with the material of the body, which makes the screw stick in place after a time, particularly with aluminium bodies. It is always a good idea to smear screw threads with synthetic grease or petroleum jelly. Do this for all garden lights, whether they will be used underwater,

Planning
the system

above: Lighting trees at the end of the garden means running cables around the garden, preferably during landscaping.

When you have decided on the subjects to light, the viewpoints, the lighting effects you want to achieve and the combinations of lamps and luminaires you wish to install, the next stage is to formalize the lighting scheme into a plan. Even an outline plan will help to get cables into the right places during landscaping.

MAKING A PLAN

Avoid lighting near utility areas or structures unless such lighting is functional and is switched on separately to ornamental lighting

Compost heap

Shed

Greenhouse

Children's play structure

Uplight feature trees only if they are of a worthwhile size when just planted

Uplighting a mature tree adds drama. Site the luminaires behind the seat

Shrub border

Seat

Moonlight from a large tree to light the path and provide dappled lighting over bench and lawn

Shrub border: light mature and architectural specimens. Avoid too much lighting in newly planted borders

Lawn with stepping stone path

Light upper pond, stream leading to waterfall and lower pond

Uplight feature urn

Light steps

Brick and stone walls can look attractive when lit – try grazing up walls or 'shadowing' young plants onto them

Terrace

Downlight dining area below pergola & to frame view of wall fountain

Dining area

Viewpoints through house windows

Wall fountain

If you are going to install a lighting system in an established garden you will need to start by drawing up a scale plan of the garden. Measure the key dimensions and draw the outline of buildings and structures, hard surfaces, such as paths, drives and patios, key focal points, such as statues or urns, water features, and feature planting or trees. You will need to include details of boundary walls and fences if you intend to run cables along them or mount transformers and other electrical equipment on them.

Mark on the plan the viewpoints by means of an arrow pointing from the window, seat, door or gateway to the feature intended to take 'centre stage' in that particular view.

USING SYMBOLS

Once you have made a plan, you can start to mark the positions of the luminaires. Use symbols so that you can easily tell when you come back to your diagram what type of luminaire you had planned in each position, what type of cabling you were using and so on. In small schemes, a simple system of letters to represent different features may suffice, or you could use a system of graphic symbols with a key so that you can tell what each represents.

In larger schemes with a greater variety of items numbered symbol listings can be used with annotation to indicate information on lamps and accessories.

WIRING AND CIRCUIT PROTECTION FOR A SMALL LOW-VOLTAGE SYSTEM

If the features you wish to light in your garden are near the house and do not need large numbers of high-powered luminaires, then the practical solution is to light your garden using a small low-voltage cable run. All such circuits must be protected by an RCD, and transformers used in the garden must be appropriate for outside use.

Switches to control
lighting circuits

Weatherproof transformer hidden behind
planting or landscape feature

Low voltage cable to
luminaires

Power from socket
or electrical outlet via
a Residual Current
Device (Earth Leakage
Circuit Breaker)

Armoured cable or mains
(line) voltage flexible
cable in conduit to
transformer positions

Cable position marked by cable warning tape.
Protect with tiles or slabs at shallow depths

Wiring a low-voltage system

In many gardens the features to be illuminated will not be close to the house, where the power source and switches are located, so the luminaires will be too far away to run on a 12-volt cable from a transformer in the house. This is because of the effect known as 'cable voltage drop', which means that the longer the cable is and the more lights that are connected to it (especially if these are higher wattage lights) the more the voltage falls in the cable. If you start with 12 volts from a transformer, there is a limit to how far you can go and to how many lights can be connected to one cable. The practical result of too much voltage drop in the cables from the transformer to a halogen lamp in a garden light is that the lamp will be dimmer than it should be and the light output will be yellow rather than white. A reduction of 10 per cent in voltage will reduce the light output of the lamp by a quarter, so a 50-watt lamp run at under 11 volts will achieve little more light output than a fully run 35-watt lamp.

Low-voltage cable runs

Regulations and local practice vary between countries, so no universal rule can be given for cable length or loading. In Europe it is usual to have more transformers spread around an area and shorter cable runs. In the United States, on the other hand, it is more usual to have fewer transformers and longer runs, often of thicker cable. Your lighting or electrical advisor will normally recommend 2.5mm² low-voltage cable to limit voltage drop to the farthest luminaire to a maximum of between 0.5 and 1.0 volt. 2.5mm² is a commonly used European size which is midway between the main US cable sizes; 12 awg (3.3mm²) and 14 awg (2.0mm²). This will maintain light output within 85 per cent of the lamp's rated performance and will maintain its colour temperature within 5 per cent of its rated temperature. Heavier-gauge cables – ones with thicker copper cores – can be used to overcome cabling problems where excavating a deep trench for a mains-voltage cable has to be avoided, but mixing too many cable sizes in one garden is rarely a good idea. It is usually best to use the common cable sizes mentioned above and to locate transformers close enough to the luminaires so that cable voltage drop remains within required limits.

If you use luminaires with lower-wattage lamps and the number of luminaires required exceeds the number that can be connected to one cable, then dividing the luminaires onto two or more cables should overcome the difficulty. The problem is avoided with many low-voltage plastic lighting kits simply because the power of the lamps used is so low that it does not lead to significant cable voltage drop.

Transformers

A transformer is an electrical or electronic device that changes voltage from one level to another. In garden lighting this is usually from the mains or utility supply voltage to 12 volts, although some low-voltage lighting runs at 24 volts. Low-voltage cable runs from the transformer to the luminaires. It usually runs under mulch and over garden structures, although it may need to be protected in a conduit, either for practical reasons or to comply with local regulations.

To minimize cable voltage drop to the luminaires, look at the location of the luminaires you have marked on your plan and identify groups of lights that can be supplied from one central transformer. Check that the transformer location is within the length of the low-voltage cable permitted. If the low-voltage cable runs are too long, divide the lights into smaller groups that can be wired from two or more transformers. In many back gardens a typical arrangement

WIRING AND CIRCUIT PROTECTION FOR A LARGER GARDEN-LIGHTING SYSTEM INVOLVING MULTIPLE CIRCUITS

Auxiliary fuseboard or distribution board for exterior circuits must include RCD protection

Separate switches for front and rear garden lighting

Mains (line) voltage cables may be armoured or flexible types in a conduit and are laid below the level where soil may be disturbed to transformers or mains (line) voltage luminaires

Powerful uplights require mains (line) voltage input

may require one transformer on each side of the garden and perhaps one transformer to cover features at the far end of the garden. A simple way of checking cable runs on a plan is to use a pair of compasses to measure the radius of a circle based on the maximum cable run from the proposed site of the transformer.

Transformers for exterior use are housed in weatherproof boxes, which come in many shapes and sizes. They can normally be hidden behind planting and landscape features. For locations where transformers cannot be hidden, special ground-burial types are available, but surface-mounted units are preferable because they are always easier to maintain. These should be installed by a professional.

Calculating transformer size

People planning a lighting system for the garden often ask how many lights can be run from a single transformer. In fact, transformers are available in a range of wattage ratings, and a more appropriate question would be: 'What size of transformer is needed to power the lights in the design? Deciding on a transformer is simply a matter of multiplying the wattage and numbers

of the lamps used in the luminaires to be connected to the transformer.

In most instances, it is sensible to allow some spare capacity within the transformer rating so that there is scope for increasing some of the lamp wattages as plants grow or for adding a luminaire in the future. Allow about 20 per cent spare capacity when you select a transformer. Transformers are usually available in 50- or 100-watt steps, so it is merely a question of choosing the next step up from the total wattage you have calculated. Avoid loading the transformer to less than two-thirds of its power rating because this can result in 'overvoltage', which reduces lamp life.

Planning a larger system

A plan for a larger system should include more detail than can easily be recorded on a single drawing or sketch plan. The basic plan should give all the essential information about the locations of luminaires, transformers, the source of power and the position of controls, in addition to details of the wiring. This can be done using graphic symbols or numbered symbols. These can be cross-referenced to notes that provide further details. The main

EXAMPLES OF CALCULATING TRANSFORMER RATINGS

TYPE OF LUMINAIRE	NUMBER OF LUMINAIRES	LAMP WATTAGE	TOTAL WATTAGE	SPARE CAPACITY	TRANSFORMER RATING (WATTS)
Example 1					
Spike-mount spotlight	3	50	150		
Wall-mounted spotlight	2	20	40		
Spreadlight	2	20	40		
Total	**7**		**230**	**+ 70**	**= 300**
Example 2					
Recessed uplight	1	75	75		
Underwater light	1	35	35		
Step light	2	20	40		
Tree-mounted downlight	1	20	20		
Total	**5**		**170**	**+ 30**	**= 200**

left: Examples of garden lighting transformers: from left – transformer in weatherproof wall-mounting box with cable input and output; transformer sealed into wall-mounting enclosures with cable entries; ground-burial transformer kit with polyurethane potting kit for on-site sealing.

schedule will list all the lighting effects and the lamps and luminaires specified. It should also define any separation of lighting onto separate circuits and provide an opportunity for noting special requirements, either for switching or for accessories. A second schedule should list the transformers in relation to the circuit to which they are connected, and detail the lights powered from each.

A larger scheme may include front and rear gardens, a pool area and a children's play area. The rear garden element may include an ornamental lighting circuit for a water feature, trees and shrubs, plus separate circuits for pathlighting, terrace lighting and wall lights on the house itself. Lighting circuits may be switched on and off separately and from different locations, which may include the sitting room and dining room, as well as weatherproof switches in the pool area. This means that the garden and pathlighting can be switched on when leaving the pool area if darkness falls while you are enjoying an evening by the pool. The pool and play area lighting may also be switched on and off at different places.

below: The ambience of this garden scene is created by using different lighting techniques to accentuate the dining area, pond and features, such as the urns and architectural plants.

Implementation and installation

above: The carefully positioned light beams have cast dramatic shadows and silhouettes on this modern architecture.

Installation of any electrical equipment in gardens is a job for a qualified electrical contractor, especially if water is involved, but understanding some of the issues which need to be considered will help you when drawing up an installation brief for your contractor that reflects your requirements. It may also help the installation to run more smoothly, and the finished scheme will certainly be more successful if you appreciate how the various parts of the project relate to one another.

Safety

Installing electricity in the garden is not a job for amateurs, and electrical equipment in the garden can be lethal if incorrectly installed or if inadequate provisions have been made in the event of an equipment fault. Water is the main threat. It can seep in through joints and gaskets; it can be drawn into electrical enclosures by capillary action; it can form from repeated condensation cycles and it can penetrate ageing materials which corrode, crack or are damaged by wildlife, pets, children, careless gardening or just time. Water conducts electricity, and the ground is usually damp to some extent or other in most countries, so that the contact of human feet with the ground is all that is needed to provide a fatal route for electrical current. Proper circuit protection for all exterior electrical services should include a residual current device (RCD), known as an earth leakage circuit breaker (ELCB) or ground fault interruptor (GFI) in some countries. This simple device ensures that the power is cut off immediately it detects a leakage of current to earth, which indicates an electrical fault potentially threatening to life. So, observe a few simple rules and keep your garden safe.

Who does what?

Bear in mind that although an electrical contractor may be qualified to install the system, few electricians have much experience of designing garden lighting systems. You may already have decided to seek the services of a garden lighting specialist to prepare the lighting design you require and to draw up the plan. You may pay a fee for this service, although some specialists will provide the design service as part of a package that includes sourcing products from manufacturers and installation. Some landscape contractors may be able to provide this service as well as lay the cables in the garden during landscape works. Finding a garden lighting specialist is becoming easier as the market grows and new companies emerge. Searching directories or asking friends and garden designers for recommendations can now be supplemented by searching the Internet under 'garden lighting' or 'landscape lighting'. Whoever you choose for help with design or installation, look for evidence of experience in testimonials, recommendations or photographs of completed projects.

Power for the system

Garden lighting is rarely installed as the only equipment that is run by electricity in a garden, and these other services must be taken into account. This does not mean that the power for all equipment must come from the same place. Lighting is slightly different in that convenience usually demands that the switches are in the house or on the patio. Most other services, such as supplies to exterior electrical sockets, sheds and irrigation controllers, are

DO	DON'T
• Employ a qualified electrical contractor for all garden electrical installations • Ensure that all exterior electrical circuits are protected by an RCD • Have your system tested by a qualified electrical contractor if you have any doubts • Turn electrical equipment off before performing any maintenance function, even just changing a lamp	• Install electrical equipment outside unless you are qualified to do so • Use switches, sockets, transformers or any other electrical devices in the garden if they are designed for interior installation • Protect electrical equipment with plastic bags or temporary wrappings as a substitute for proper weatherproof enclosures

either unswitched or, like timers to control fountain pumps, which may need to be turned off at night, are switched by other means.

It may not always be possible to provide power from the house because existing hard landscaping would make it difficult and disruptive to lay cables. Sometimes the power for the lighting is taken from a supply in the garage, pool house, greenhouse or other outbuilding, and control may be provided by remote controls or automatic devices.

Power for simple systems

Many systems need only a limited amount of power. A small system with a few spotlights for ornamental effect, an additional path or patio lighting circuit and a low-power pump for a water feature will consume less than 5 amps of power. These can usually be wired as a spur from an electrical socket, via an RCD, a small switch panel and junction box to connect the exterior cables.

Power for larger systems

When lighting is provided for a large property, the total exterior electrical load can be both high and complex, including lighting, water pumps and irrigation systems as well as electrical supplies for pools, outbuildings and electric gates. The amount of power required usually dictates that the electrical source for exterior circuits should come from the main electrical supply, preferably via a separate distribution board. This will contain residual current devices (RCDs) to provide essential safety protection and miniature circuit breakers (MCBs) to provide protection against overload and short-circuit.

In very large installations, where the house has a three-phase electrical supply, there are a number of different options. The exterior circuits may be taken from one phase; from selected circuits of different phases to balance the load; or, where the total amount of electrical power required is very high, from a separate three-phase supply. The advantage of taking exterior circuits from the incoming supply is that the circuit

protection is separate for interior and exterior circuits, so that an exterior fault in a luminaire, pump cable or garden socket will not make interior circuits trip.

Laying cables

Providing cables for complex electrical systems in large gardens should be done by an electrical engineer. Although some general guidelines apply to all gardens, these may be affected by local regulations and practices. For example, in Britain steel wire-armoured cables are usually used for mains voltage wiring that is buried in the ground, but in other countries flexible cable in conduit is more common.

The amount of mains-voltage cable required for garden lighting will be reduced if a low-voltage system is chosen. Flexible low-voltage cables can be run from transformers that are hidden behind plants and landscape features so that all that is needed is a relatively simple infrastructure of mains cabling to the transformers. Mains-voltage cables must be buried so deeply that they are unlikely to be disturbed by subsequent gardening – depths of 30–45cm (12–18in) below a lawn and 45–60cm (18–24in) below cultivated ground are appropriate. Using a simple mains-voltage cable layout will reduce the amount of digging required. This can be an important factor in an established garden, and digging a trench around the edge of a lawn is generally easier than through mature, well-grown borders.

Apart from the safety considerations of inappropriate cabling, which your contractor will help you to avoid, many misconceptions about electrical wiring based on a limited understanding of household appliances, are transferred to the garden. The most usual mistakes are to have mains-voltage cables that are too small for the load or that do not cater for a sufficient number of circuits.

Cable size

The most common misconception is that the gauge of wiring used for the interior lighting circuit or for the table lamps in the sitting room is adequate outside.

Unfortunately, this ignores the fact that cable voltage drop is often a more important factor in cable selection than the amount of electrical current it has to carry. Indoor cable runs are relatively short, but the amount of lighting in a garden can exceed that on a lighting circuit in the house. For example, 1.5mm^2 three-core cable is the minimum size of cable for lighting a small garden, but expecting such a cable to carry power to light large trees 100m (110yds) from the house is unrealistic. The mains-voltage cable size must be calculated according to the length of the cable run, so if your garden is anything other than a small one, upgrade to the next cable size, 2.5mm^2 or even 4mm^2.

Too few cables

The other common mistake is thinking in terms of a single electrical supply into the garden when you actually require several electrical services. One three-core mains cable may be fine for running the fountain pump during the day and the evening before you switch off at night, but if you wish to operate the lighting and the pump separately, you will need to have one three-core cable for each function. This also applies to other services, such as power to the shed or the swimming pool. In addition, if you wish to switch on lighting selectively on separate circuits, you will need to lay enough cables to do so. This can either be separate three-core cables to each transformer location on each circuit, or a multicore cable to cater for enough circuits. The only other possible approach is to convert a single electricity supply into multiple functions by using remote or automatic controls, but this is often less convenient and more expensive to install than the familiar switch on the wall.

LAYING CABLES

Laying electrical cables in the ground may be subject to specific regulations in different countries. The aim is to ensure that the cables are buried deeply enough in the ground to avoid any disturbance likely to occur. Where armoured cables can be buried at adequate depth, they can be laid in a buffer layer of sand and covered with cable warning tape. Where it is not possible to bury the cables deeply enough because of the presence of tree roots or unsuitable ground conditions, extra mechanical protection around the cables will be required. This is usually in the form of plastic ducts or conduits through which the cables are run. For extra protection, the cable or duct could also be covered with a layer of tiles.

Cable warning tape

Armoured cable laid direct into sand

Buffer layer of sand

duct

Cable warning tape

Buffer layer of sand

Cables protected in duct

Installing cable in new gardens

Because low-voltage systems require a comparatively simple mains-voltage cable layout, they are usually easier to introduce into gardens that are to be newly landscaped. It is sometimes difficult to imagine how the garden will look from a two-dimensional plan, and if your garden is being landscaped professionally you might find it easier to leave the final design of the lighting scheme until the garden is complete, but to lay cables while the other work is being carried out.

Some wiring must be specific – for example, for uplighting large trees (which is beyond the scope of low-voltage equipment anyway) and for any lighting that needs to be built into walls or paving as part of the construction process – but the remainder of the system can be finalized later as long as the mains-voltage cable infrastructure has been installed during landscaping. If this is done, it is necessary to prepare only an outline lighting design to establish the transformer positions, numbers of circuits, power source and switching requirements. The result is a cable plan, which can be implemented by landscapers during the construction work. The lighting scheme can be finalized later.

Controlling the system

As well as providing enough cables to provide the power needed in the garden, you should also consider the type of switches that you need and the most appropriate places to install them.

Manual switching

For most systems, a simple switch on the wall is all that is needed. We can use it to switch lights and equipment on and off when we feel like it and have selected lighting on separate switches if we have planned it that way. In most gardens that probably means having one switch for the ornamental garden lighting circuit, one for the downlighting over the pergola or patio, and one for the wall lights on the rear of the house. Extra switches allow us to switch security floodlights on manually for reassurance when we hear a noise outside, and off again so they do

TYPICAL CONTROLS FOR VARIOUS TYPES OF LIGHTING CIRCUIT	
TYPES OF LIGHT	**TYPES OF CONTROL**
Security lighting	Operated by passive infra-red movement detectors; override enables lighting to be switched on or off manually; separate control panel for a multi-zone system, possibly linked to alarm system
Driveway lighting	Photocell for dawn to dusk operation; timer/photocell or solar dial timer for automatic operation without seasonal adjustment; an alternative to security lighting with movement detectors
Entrance lighting	Manually switched or automatic operation as for driveway lighting
Façade lighting	Manually switched or automatic operation as for driveway lighting
Ornamental lighting	Manually switched by wall-mounted switches or remote controls
Pathlighting	Manually switched in rear gardens; automatic operation as for driveway lighting in front gardens; two-way switching may be required in larger gardens for paths linking pool areas and so on
Patio/terrace lighting	Manually switched; dimmers for enhanced control of ambient lighting in intimate settings
Task lighting	Weatherproof switch for barbecue lighting; local switches for tennis court lighting, etc
Gazebo lighting	Local switch inside gazebo for internal downlighting; exterior lighting on ornamental circuit
Pool lighting	Manual switching on same panel as poolside and pool-house lighting

not interfere with more subtle lighting. Switches are best sited near to the windows from which the view is seen or the doors through which the garden is entered – the conservatory, lounge or dining room for the back-garden lighting and the entrance hall for the front garden.

Using contactors makes it possible to control the lighting system from several locations or for different types of controls to be used together – for example, linking driveway lighting to security lighting circuits after an automatic timed period and providing manual override facilities.

Dimmers

The use of dimmers has increased dramatically in recent years and in large gardens they can take the form of sophisticated 'scene-setting' systems in which a computerized controller will set several lighting circuits to create functional or mood-related lighting set-ups in reception rooms. Dimmers are not generally recommended for garden lighting, for several reasons. If both the garden and the garden lighting system have been well designed, the lighting should not need significant adjustment to its brightness to provide interest all year round. Adjustments to brightness can be made by changing lamp beams and wattages to achieve the correct balance in the design. Some types of garden lighting – metal halide lighting for large trees and compact fluorescent lamps in wall lights, for example – are not suitable for use with dimmers and can be damaged by them, and special types of dimmers must be used with low-voltage lighting. In addition, simple wall dimmers are limited in power rating to under 400 watts, which is less than the power of a typical garden-lighting circuit, except in a very small garden.

Small, intimate spaces where the lighting level can dramatically affect the ambience of the occasion are an exception – courtyard, balcony and roof gardens and al fresco dining areas are examples, especially where dimming the lighting can enable you to see a vista beyond.

Remote controls

If power has to be taken from a location where switches would be inconvenient, fitting a remote control unit is one way of making the system easier to use. Radio remote controls are now available in FM long-range versions that are capable of switching on lighting up to 300m (325yds) away. This is a theoretical 'line of sight' range, which is reduced by the presence of large trees, metal structures and buildings.

Photocells and timers

Photocells are electronic devices that sense ambient daylight levels and switch on lighting when it gets dark and switches it off again at dawn. This is a simple method of automatic control if you want lighting on all night. Check that photocells are suitable for use with compact fluorescent lamps if you wish to use these for their long lamp life.

You can use a photocell in conjunction with a timer so that the photocell switches the on lighting when dusk falls, and the timer switches off the lighting at a chosen time. This is a popular method of control where all-night lighting is not required. Timers usually have the facility for manual override and are available in both 24-hour and 7-day versions. Special types, which automatically adjust for seasonal changes, are available.

Movement detectors

Movement detectors are normally associated with security lighting or alarm systems. Passive infra-red detectors seek movement by monitoring heat sources – usually body heat or heat from vehicles. Beam detectors of the type commonly used with electric gates may also be used to switch on lighting. You may wish to have this method of control because it provides convenient automatic switching without expensive or disruptive wiring. Lighting the way from a garage to the side door of the house so that the light switches on when you step into range and off again after a timed period is a good example of this type of system.

Glossary

Absorption: The amount of light taken in by a surface instead of being reflected.

Accent Lighting: The highlighting of individual features.

Adaptation: The process which takes place as the eye adjusts to variations in brightness within its field of vision.

Ambient Lighting: Soft, indirect illumination.

Beam Angle: The angle of coverage of the pattern of light produced by a reflector lamp or by the combination of a lamp and a reflector.

Black Mirror Effect: The effect which makes window glass a dark reflective mirror at night.

Cable Voltage Drop: A reduction in electrical pressure in a cable resulting from increasing distance from the power source or increased power (wattage or current) drawn along the cable. Higher wattage lamps positioned further away from a transformer will experience reduced voltage, which reduces light output and can inhibit efficient operation of the halogen cycle.

Colour Rendering: A comparative term to describe how well a lamp illuminates an object's colours compared with daylight.

Contrast: The difference in appearance of two parts of a visual field seen simultaneously or successively.

Diffused Lighting: Illumination which appears to come from many directions, or at least is not dependent on a light beam from one direction.

Diffusion Filter: A frosted or opal glass lens that is used to widen or soften light output.

Dimming: The control of the light output from the light source by electrical or resistive methods.

Directional Lighting: Lighting designed to illuminate an object or surface predominantly from a chosen direction.

Direct Lighting: Lighting in which the greater part of the illumination reaches a surface directly, i.e. without reflection from other surfaces.

Disability Glare: Glare which impairs the ability to see detail.

Discharge lamp: A lamp in which bright, energy-efficient light is produced by electrically exciting pressurised gas in a bulb.

Discomfort Glare: Glare which causes visual discomfort.

Fibre Optic Lighting: A system of projecting light along a bundle of optical glass fibres.

Filter: A glass or metal accessory which alters the characteristics (shape, colour etc.) of light beam patterns.

Fluorescent lamp: A lamp in which energy-efficient light is produced by electrically exciting a phosphor coating on the inside surface of a glass tube or container.

Glare: The discomfort or impairment of vision experienced when parts of the visual field are excessively bright in relation to the general surroundings.

Illuminance: The concept of illumination falling on to a surface. The unit of measurement in Europe is the lux which is 1 lumen per square metre.

Illumination: The process of lighting an object or surface.

Indirect Lighting: Lighting in which the greater part of the illumination reaches a surface only after reflection from other surfaces.

Incandescent lamp: A lamp in which light is produced by a filament (usually made of tungsten) heated to incandescence by the passage of an electric current through it.

Kelvin: Degrees Kelvin is a measure of the colour temperature of light.

Lamp: The lighting industry term for a light bulb.

Light bulb: Layman's term for a lamp, i.e. a glass container with a coating, filament or gas which glows when electricity is applied.

Line Voltage: Alternative term to describe mains voltage for household electricity supply. *see* Mains Voltage.

Louvre: An open grid of translucent or opaque elements attached to a luminaire in such a position that the lamps cannot be seen directly above a given angle, normally the maximum beam angle of the lamps fitted.

Luminaire: An apparatus which includes all the components necessary for fixing and protecting lamps and for connecting them to the supply circuit. Luminaire has superseded the term lighting fitting or light fixture in the lighting industry.

Lux: The SI unit of illuminance, equal to 1 lumen per square metre.

Mains Voltage: The voltage at which household electricity is normally supplied. Single phase mains voltage in Europe is harmonized at 230 volts. The standard in North America is 120 volts.

Mercury Vapour Lamp: High intensity discharge lamp in which light is emitted mainly as a result of electrical excitation of mercury compounds within a bulb.

Metal Halide Lamp: High intensity discharge lamp in which light is emitted as a result of electrical excitation of metal halides within a bulb.

Mirror Reflector Lamp: A type of reflector lamp with a mirror-finish reflector to control and direct the light output. Size is denoted in eighths of an inch in diameter; e.g. an MR16 lamp is 2 inches (50mm) in diameter.

PAR lamp: Reflector lamp with a parabolic aluminised reflector. Size is denoted in eighths of an inch in diameter; e.g. a PAR38 lamp is 4.75 inches (120mm) in diameter.

Reflectance: The ratio of the amount of light reflected from a surface to the illuminance falling upon it.

Reflector: A device for controlling the light emitted from a lamp by reflection at suitably shaped surfaces, normally conical or bowl-shaped for spotlights.

Reflector Lamp: An incandescent or discharge lamp in which part of the bulb, suitably shaped, is coated internally with a reflecting material which partly controls the distribution of light emitted from the lamp.

Spread Lens: A glass lens used to diffuse and widen or elongate light beam patterns.

Transformer: A magnetic or electronic device which increases or decreases the voltage of alternating current (AC) electricity; mainly used for low voltage lighting.

Tungsten Halogen Lamp: A tungsten filament lamp containing halogens.

Voltage: A measurement of electrical pressure through a cable or electrical apparatus

Wattage: The power rating, measured in watts, of a lamp or electrical apparatus.

Index

Acknowledgements

In Source Order

Emap Gardening Picture Library 23 top, 24 bottom, 39 top.

Elizabeth Whiting Associates/Tim Street Porter 49 bottom.

Andrea Jones/Garden Exposures/Trevyn McDowell's roof garden, Clerkenwell, courtesy Channel 4 series 'Garden Doctors' 4–5, 52 top.

Garden Picture Library/Andrew Payne 91, /Gary Rogers 117 bottom, /Ron Sutherland/ Eco Design, Melbourne 66 bottom.

Jerry Harpur/Design: Stephen Crisp, London 48 top, /Design: Grover Dear, Hong Kong 1, 38, /Design: Topher Delaney, San Francisco 43, 50 top, /Design: Sonny Garcia, San Francisco 6, 97, 101, /Design: Luciano Giubbilei, London 9, 34, 41 top, /Mr & Mrs Lerner, California 2, 37, /Longwood, Pennsylvania 55 top, /Design: Made Wijaya, Bali, Indonesia 27 bottom, /Design: Camille Muller, Paris 102, /David Pearson, London 39 bottom, 77, /Design: Dan Pearson, London 118.

Marcus Harpur/Princes Trust RHS Chelsea 2000 25 bottom.

The Interior Archive/Ed Reeve/Architect: Adajaye & Russell 27 top.

Lighting for Gardens/ www.lightingforgardens.co.uk 50 bottom, 51 top, 64, 105, 107 top, 107 bottom, 108, 109, 110, 111 top, 111 bottom, 117 top.

Marianne Majerus/Design: Jill Billington 45 top, /Design: George Carter, The Christie Sculpture Garden, RHS Chelsea 1999 46 top, /Design: John Sarbutt 32, /Hotel Tresanton, St Mawes, Cornwall 15, 20, 40, /Design: Mathew Vincent 12, 104, /Design: Stephen Woodhams 7 top, 90 bottom.

Megabay Lighting Enterprises/ www.megabay.com (4 Development Court, Caloundra, Queensland, 4551, Australia) 30, 62, 67, 88, 92, 99.

Clive Nichols Photography/Garden & Security Lighting 35 top, 56, 112, /Trevyn McDowell & Paul Thompson 90 top, 96, /Design: Natural & Oriental Water Gardens/ Garden & Security Lighting 11, 21, 55 bottom, 63, 83, /The Nichols Gdn, Reading/ Garden & Security Lighting 57 top, /Peter Reid. 45 bottom, /spidergarden.com/Chelsea 2000 54, /Stephen Woodhams 31.

Louis Poulsen/Tony Craddock/ tcr-uk@lpmail.com (Surrey Business Park, Weston Road, Epsom, Surrey, KT17 1JG, UK) 13, 24–25, 48 bottom, 49 top, 65, 69, 93, 94, 95.

John Raine 7 bottom, 8 top, 8 bottom, 10 top right, 10 bottom left, 14, 16, 17, 19, 23 bottom, 26, 28, 29, 33, 35 bottom, 36, 41 bottom, 42 top, 42 bottom, 44 top, 44 bottom right, 46 bottom, 47, 51 bottom, 52 bottom, 57 bottom, 61 top, 61 bottom, 66 top, 68 left, 68 right, 73, 74 top, 74 bottom, 75 left, 75 right, 76, 78 top, 78 bottom, 79, 82 top, 82 bottom, 84 top, 84 bottom, 85, 86, 87, 89 top, 89 bottom, 98, 100, 103.

Project Editor: Sarah Ford
Editors: Lydia Darbyshire, Meg Sanders, Cathy Lowne
Index: Indexing Specialists

Executive Art Editor: Geoff Fennell
Designer: Emily Wilkinson

Production Controller: Lucy Woodhead

Picture Research: Zoë Holtermann